"Even the title has got it right!"

—Norman R. Augustine, President (retired), Lockheed Martin Corporation

"The most truthful, straight-talk book on managing people to come along in eons. This is an exceptional tool for business."

—Harvey MacKay, author of *Swim with the Sharks without Being Eaten Alive*

"One of the very best organized, thought out, planned, and written books on any business subject I have read."

—Stanley Bass, Human Resources Consultant, Stan Bass Consulting

"An excellent read; it certainly confirms my real-life experience of progress over time at Verizon."

—Mike Steiner, Director, Enterprise Solutions Group, Verizon

"Finally, the truth about empowerment!"

—Jack Canfield, coauthor of *Chicken Soup for the Soul*

"This book is now ... ers. You can't succeed toda ... oyees."

—John S ... der Joe's

"The principles outlined are essential if you are to achieve true empowerment."

—H. Eugene Blattman, President & CEO (retired), McCormick & Company, Inc.

"The message is clear, to the point, and right on target."

—Joseph Bode, Joseph J. Bode & Company

"I found the book was to the point and hit the nail on the head about information sharing."

—Robert S. Argabright, II, President and General Manager (formerly), Chesapeake Packaging Company

"Succinctly captures the critical elements of empowerment in a brilliantly simple format!"

—Peter B. Grazier, President, Teambuilding, Inc.

"The authors show that empowerment is more than an empty promise. A must-read for liberating the leader within people."

—Barry Z. Posner, coauthor of *The Leadership Challenge*

"The framework is perfect, clear, and concise."

—JoAnne Pitera, Organizational Effectiveness Consultant

"The material is most readable, and the key points are presented well for retention and use."

—Mike Perry, Human Resources Director, DuPont Corporation

"Very readable. Straightforward. The authors have hit the bull's eye on empowerment."

—John Coleman, CSX Corporation

"Empowerment is such an important topic. The great thing about this book is that it supplies a Game Plan for getting there."

—Bruce Dalgleish, General Mills Restaurants

"Finally, the definitive book on empowerment and productivity, profound but simple to implement."

—Shaun Conroy, VP Sales & Customer Service, NewsWest

"I could not agree more with what this fantastic little book says about how mistakes empower people. Indeed, every 'misteak' is an opportunity to increase competence and empowerment."

—John C. Maxwell, author of *Failing Forward*

"If you seriously want to unleash the people power of your organization, this book is a must. Simple and profound; all you add is courage and discipline, and you'll find it really works."

—Tom Muccio, President,
Global Customer Teams, Procter & Gamble

"This engaging book makes clear that the real power in an organization is within its people. By learning to release that power an organization can be a powerful force in the business world."

—Mark Robbins, Director,
Professional Development, Robbins-Gioia, Inc.

"It's a fun read and the principles are spot on!"

—James M. Kouzes, coauthor of *The Leadership Challenge*

EMPOWERMENT

TAKES MORE THAN A MINUTE

SECOND EDITION

EMPOWERMENT
TAKES MORE THAN A MINUTE

SECOND EDITION

Ken Blanchard
Coauthor of *The One Minute Manager*

John P. Carlos

Alan Randolph

Berrett-Koehler Publishers, Inc.
San Francisco

Berrett-Koehler Publishers, Inc.
235 Montgomery Street, Suite 650
San Francisco, CA 94104
Tel: (415) 288-0260 Fax: (415) 362-2512 www.bkconnection.com

ORDERING INFORMATION

Quantity sales. Special discounts are available on quantity purchases by corporations, associations, and others. For details, contact the "Special Sales Department" at the Berrett-Koehler address above.

Individual sales. Berrett-Koehler publications are available through most bookstores. They can also be ordered direct from Berrett-Koehler: Tel: (800) 929-2929; Fax: (802) 864-7626; www.bkconnection.com

Orders for college textbook/course adoption use. Please contact Berrett-Koehler: Tel: (800) 929-2929; Fax: (802) 864-7626.

Orders by U.S. trade bookstores and wholesalers. Please contact Ingram Publisher Services, Tel: (800) 509-4887; Fax: (800) 838-1149; E-mail: customer.service@ingrampublisherservices.com; or visit www.ingrampublisherservices.com/Ordering for details about electronic ordering.

Printed in the United States of America

Berrett-Koehler books are printed on long-lasting acid-free paper. When it is available, we choose paper that has been manufactured by environmentally responsible processes. These may include using trees grown in sustainable forests, incorporating recycled paper, minimizing chlorine in bleaching, or recycling the energy produced at the paper mill.

Library of Congress Cataloging-in-Publication Data

Blanchard, Kenneth H.
Empowerment takes more than a minute / Ken Blanchard, John P. Carlos, Alan Randolph.—2nd ed.
p. cm.
Includes bibliographical references and index.
ISBN: 978-1-57675-153-4
1. Employee empowerment. 2. Delegation of authority. 3. Decentralization in management. I. Carlos, John P. II. Randolph, W. Alan. III. Title.

HD50.5 .B55 2001
658.4'02—dc21 2001035873

Second Edition
12 11 10 09 08 15 14 13 12 11 10 9 8

to...

Dorothy Blanchard
Donald L. and Isabella Carlos
Wallace Randolph

who taught us so much about being empowered

Contents

Preface

Few changes in business have been so well received yet so problematic as the movement to create empowered, employee-driven work environments. Empowerment offers the potential for tapping into a wellspring of underutilized human capacity that must be harnessed if organizations are to survive in today's increasingly complex and dynamic world.

Empowered employees benefit the organization and themselves. They have a greater sense of purpose in their jobs and lives, and their involvement translates directly into continuous improvement in the workplace systems and processes. In an empowered organization, employees bring their best ideas and initiatives to the workplace with a sense of excitement, ownership, and pride. In addition, they act with responsibility and put the best interests of the organization first.

The traditional management model of the manager in control and employees under control is no longer effective. To create an empowered workplace, management's role in organizations must move from a command-and-control mind-set to a responsibility-oriented and supportive environment in which all employees have the opportunity to do their best.

Shifting to an empowerment philosophy calls for changes in most aspects of an organization. Both managers and employees must learn, first, not to be bureaucratic and, second, to be empowered. Unfortunately, many managers do not understand that empowerment involves releasing the power people already have, nor do they understand how to navigate the journey to empowerment.

Empowerment Takes More Than a Minute is a how-to book that guides readers step-by-step through one manager's struggle to discover the three essential keys to empowerment. By following the manager's odyssey to the Land of Empowerment, readers discover that they can take the same journey, which, like any heroic journey, is filled with paradox, challenge, and fitful stops and starts. *Empowerment Takes More Than a Minute* provides practical and simple concepts that CEOs, COOs, CIOs, and managers and employees at all levels in organizations both public and private can apply to their particular situations.

Though many managers have dismissed empowerment as another passing gimmick, we find that people in organizations are naturally attracted to the idea of enhanced involvement at all levels. Also, we personally have seen organizations succeed with empowerment. For more than fifteen years, we have worked extensively with a wide variety of domestic and multinational companies that were trying to create empowered workplaces. These companies have taught us a great deal about what empowerment is and how to create it. They haven't always known the answers to the questions raised by empowerment, and neither have we. Quite the contrary, it has been through missteps that we have learned the three keys to empowerment presented in this book.

In this second edition to *Empowerment Takes More Than a Minute*, we provide a new introduction that explains how empowerment has moved beyond the fad stage and become essential for effective organizations in today's dynamic and complex world. We have also updated the text and characters for today's technologically sophisticated business world. Finally, we added an epilogue that reinforces the difficulty of moving to empowerment and suggests some tools to help managers and team members succeed in the journey.

Empowerment is definitely achievable, but the journey is not for the weak in spirit. For those of you who undertake it, we urge you to stay the course. We know that your path can be made easier if you start with and stick to the three keys of empowerment explained in *Empowerment Takes More Than a Minute.*

Good luck on your journey.

Ken Blanchard *John Carlos* *Alan Randolph*
Fall 2001

Introduction to the Second Edition

One of the joys of writing a business best-seller is the feedback and validation you receive for the messages in the book. Unfortunately, one of the problems with writing about empowerment is that too many organizations have dismissed it as a fad that cannot be of much help in today's high-technology business world.

We disagree and believe that, if anything, empowerment is even more necessary today than it was in the past. While information technology and the internet have opened global doors and allowed for rapid response to the market, they have also raised the bar for success and effectiveness. As numerous business failures have proven, slick ideas and revenue generation do not guarantee company success. Unless the innovative ideas are significant and costs can simultaneously be controlled, a company's existence will be short-lived.

Doing business today means succeeding in a world that is increasingly complex and more dynamic. The global economy offers access to many new markets, but it also demands an understanding of cultural differences and a constant vigilance for competition that can come from anywhere in the world. The technological environment of business makes it increasingly easy to change products, services, pricing, and advertising strategies but at the same time affords the opportunity for compounding errors at a dizzying pace. Couple these factors with the diversity of the workforce and the marketplace, the call for environmental responsibility, the stress on ethical behaviors, and the rapid changes in politics and economics throughout the world, and you have a business environment that demands better utilization of the human magnificence that lies in wait in every organization.

Too many business leaders give lip service to human talent as the underutilized asset in their companies, while they continue to look for answers in technology and spreadsheets. We would encourage business leaders to add to their list of solutions the wealth of talent that lies in their people. Indeed, empowerment relies on an explicit recognition that people in organizations have tremendous power in their experience, knowledge, and internal motivation. When this power is released and directed toward the challenges businesses face, it is truly astonishing the results that can be achieved. Empowered organizations are filled with engaged, involved people who can greatly help in achieving flexibility, customer responsiveness, innovation, and financial success in a challenging and competitive business environment. We believe empowerment is the key to integrating technology, financial acumen, and human innovation.

As numerous companies have found, empowerment is not flawed. Yes, some successful leaders call it entrepreneurship, some call it ownership, some call it engagement, and some simply call it involvement. But the common theme is that they recognize the need to *release the knowledge, experience and motivation power within people for astonishing results.*

Granted, empowerment can be a difficult concept to appreciate fully—and even more difficult to implement. Too many business leaders think that the journey to empowerment should be quick and easy. All management has to do is give it a nudge, and employees will jump on the opportunity. Unfortunately, changing the history and assumptions in people and organizations is much more challenging. What we knew before writing the first edition of this book and what has been confirmed by numerous readers, worldwide, is that the change to empowerment is *hard*!

But it is certainly possible. We have been encouraged to find a number of organizations that have made empowerment part of their culture.

For example, one specialty retail food company, Trader Joe's, has made significant strides toward creating a culture of empowerment. By giving people more information, greater autonomy, and more responsibility, they have been able to utilize the collective power in their people to achieve annual sales growth exceeding

26 percent. Sales per store increased by 10 percent per year while the number of stores increased by almost 100 percent, and overall sales increased in excess of 500 percent over an eight-year period. Their president, John Shields, said it well: "You can't successfully run stores spread over a growing number of states without empowered employees."

And a surprising organization that has made real progress with empowerment is the Collections Division of the Los Angeles Field Office of the IRS—yes, the IRS. And if they can do it, certainly your organization can, too. By recognizing the talents of all staff and stressing a message of service, they have focused the efforts of the entire staff. The management team of Art Hylton, Steve Jensen, and Rich Morgante conducted a series of twelve town hall meetings to share the message that everyone had to look at his or her own behavior first. By conducting a service assessment and discussing the results, the leaders reduced the existing "we-they" attitude and provided a target on which everyone, working in teams, could focus. Their journey is still in progress, but the results so far suggest they may just make it to the Land of Empowerment. We wish them well in their continued efforts.

By *Sharing Information*, *Declaring the Boundaries for Autonomy*, and *Creating Self-Managed Teams*, these organizations and many others have made substantial progress toward empowerment and toward addressing the challenges of doing business today. We want to challenge all companies and their leaders to make the same commitment to empowerment.

To ignore empowerment is not simply to ignore a fad. It is to ignore the very tools that may make your organization successful today and into the future.

We hope that you will read this book with these thoughts in mind and that if you are serious about making the journey, you will use as a guide our second book, *The Three Keys to Empowerment: Release the Power within People for Astonishing Results* (1999). You may also find useful for teams in your organization the ten-part discussion guide titled *Power Up for Team Results* (2000) (both the book and booklets are published by Berrett-Koehler in San Francisco).

We know that the challenges of changing to empowerment are many and that the journey is difficult, but we also know that the results at the end are more than worth the effort—higher quality, better service, more competitiveness, lower costs, greater flexibility in addressing customer needs, and people who feel engaged and magnificent.

So we wish you the conviction to work toward empowerment, and we hope that along the way you will enjoy the process of change. Empowerment is a beautiful place to be, and the process of getting there is filled not only with challenges but also with many rewards. Enjoy and empower!

Ken Blanchard *John Carlos* *Alan Randolph*
Fall 2001

EMPOWERMENT

TAKES MORE THAN A MINUTE

SECOND EDITION

THE CHALLENGE

THE RAIN beat down steadily. Occasionally the wind threw great splashes against the executive office windows. The sound brought a smile to Michael Hobbs's face. It made him reflect on the beating he was taking as president and CEO of a midsize, once-successful, home products company.

Michael had taken over leadership a little over a year ago, and he had instinctively done his usual thing—seize the checkbook and centralize all decision making. He had developed quite a reputation since his MBA program as a dynamic, high-energy manager. His belief was that lack of leadership at the top was usually the cause of a company's problems. As a hands-on manager, it didn't take him long to address that void. He was decisive and in charge, but for some reason his approach was not working this time.

Another sheet of rain blasted the office windows, rousing Michael from his trance. He looked up at the sign on his desk given to him by the consultant his board had recommended he should hire. The sign was really starting to bother him, but he didn't have the nerve to take it down. It read:

> The kind
> of thinking
> that led
> to past success
> will not lead
> to future
> success.

He recalled the consultant putting the sign there after giving Michael and his management team the results of a study conducted on their industry, their competition, and the company itself. It reminded Michael of a painfully obvious fact that the study had confirmed: *Management's thinking is the first thing that has to change.*

The board had insisted that Michael use this consultant, because they felt the home products industry was changing so rapidly that he could no longer figure everything out alone. They felt he needed help. Michael vehemently disagreed, yet he had to admit that the consultant's study did bring up some interesting points.

In no uncertain terms, the study warned that the company would be crushed by its competition unless all thinking, structure, processes, and action conformed to four critical organizational attributes. The company needed to be better at being:

1. Customer and quality driven
2. Revenue- and cost-effective
3. Fast and flexible in responding to market changes
4. Continually innovating

Now, as he had so many times before, Michael mentally reviewed each item on that list.

1. CUSTOMER AND QUALITY DRIVEN

No one needed to convince Michael that in today's market, success begins with customers. But somehow, many companies had lost sight of the need to focus on quality and dependability, as perceived by the customers. The do-it-yourself explosion had made him and others feel that they only had to get the new products out quickly to keep pace with competition (or, better yet, stay ahead). But now quality was again being thrust into the equation. Change had come with blinding speed. With the sophistication of today's customers and the variety of products available on the global market, the study insisted that any organization not responsive to customers' wants and needs was doomed to be second-rate or soon out of business! And he did not want his company to be one of those out of business soon.

2. REVENUE- AND COST-EFFECTIVE

The importance of this attribute didn't surprise Michael, either. He had always been one to focus on controlling costs. Too many companies had begun to believe during the technology revolution that all that mattered was top-line revenue. How wrong they had been. Cost increases, together with fierce pricing battles, had forced companies to shave margins to a fraction of what they had been. And it was easy to let margins slip into negative territory. Now was clearly a time when companies had to build revenue streams in ways that were also cost-effective.

3. FAST AND FLEXIBLE IN RESPONDING TO MARKET CHANGES

The third attribute reminded Michael of just how difficult it had become to manage effectively in a global economy. Markets could shift so quickly with customer demands being driven from all corners of the world. Competitors could appear from any direction with technological ease. And if your company did not respond, revenue and market share could drop drastically.

The study pointed out that rapidly changing customer needs and wants made cumbersome decision making and implementation processes deadly for a company. In the time it took to collect information for his management team to make decisions and then move the decisions through the company hierarchy, the customer would be gone. On the other hand, if he let people throughout the organization act freely, chaos would follow and costs would go through the roof. His concern reflected a real dilemma for the company.

Customers wanted their contacts in the company—front-line employees—to make decisions, solve problems, and take action right on the spot. Clearly, quicker, on-the-spot decisions were better, and Michael was reluctantly beginning to accept that point. But he wondered how he as CEO could keep control of such a rapidly changing organization. He was afraid his people would make too many mistakes that would cost the company too much money.

4. CONTINUALLY INNOVATING

Everywhere Michael turned, he heard that lifelong learning had to become a norm in his company. Everyone in the company would have to embrace the vision of a corporation that would be better today than it was yesterday and better tomorrow than today. Michael knew that would be a difficult task—creating an organization that would steadily and consistently outdo itself. But even more difficult would be focusing the power of people to innovate continually. He knew that without innovation a company is dead today!

Michael was growing more anxious by the moment. He realized the consultant's recommendations were right. He knew that if the company were to survive, he would have to create an organization that was simultaneously *customer and quality driven, revenue- and cost-effective, fast and flexible, and continually innovating*. But how?

He kept hearing that he needed to find ways to engage people throughout the company. They had to become owners and entrepreneurs in spirit. He had to release all the untapped creative energy of the people in the company and yet not lose control of the company. People had to be expected to take responsibility for their actions and decisions, while making full use of their skills and abilities. They had to be engaged in addressing all four of these attributes for success.

Empowerment, thought Michael. That's what some people say we need, but he felt he had already tried to empower people with little success. Six months ago he had reduced some of the layers of management in the company and put out a statement that everyone was authorized to make decisions that would help them better serve customers, control costs, increase revenues, and keep the company innovating. He had told his management team to follow up with this change in decision making.

Six months, Michael mused, yet nothing seems any different. As he looked out at the driving rain, he wondered, Where is the spirit of responsibility at work? Where is all that desire to make a contribution?

The sad truth was that throughout the organization people were acting no differently than they had when the company was a multilayered bureaucracy. Few people seemed willing to step up to the plate and take on the challenge. And where some people had taken action, they had often created problems due to their lack of understanding of the implications of their actions. They had had to be pulled back a little. A pall of reluctance hung over the workplace.

As Michael took the pulse of the company—meeting with employee groups, asking questions of the front line—he had yet to see people *acting* empowered. In fact, they went about their business in the same manner as when the company was dominated by its deadly bureaucratic mind-set. With all the talk about the need for empowerment, Michael thought the shift would happen spontaneously once he authorized people to make more decisions on their own. Obviously, that was not the case.

Everywhere Michael looked, employees' faces were masks of denial. He sensed that to them, the word *empowerment* was just that, a word—the *E* word. It was driving him crazy! And it was not helping his company, either.

He wondered if empowerment was just another buzzword. Or was there something about it that he just did not understand? On the surface it seemed people would want to use their talents and have the freedom to make decisions. They said they wanted to be more involved! So what was wrong? He had to find out before the company sank any deeper.

MICHAEL happened to notice an article sitting on his desk. The title caught his attention: "Empowerment Takes More Than a Minute." In spite of his recent skepticism, this title intrigued him and he started reading the article. The author insisted that empowerment works, but it takes courage and time to get there. The article stated that you can't tell people to act empowered and expect them to just do it—exactly what he had done six months ago. If they have little or no past experience or involvement in decision making, they won't know what to do. They may talk like they want to make more decisions about their work, but they will not be comfortable with the downside risk of responsibility.

Citing an example of one company's success in empowering its people, the article went on to rave about the turnaround of a communications hardware company that had been caught napping by the advent of the exploding communications technology demands. The manager, some guy named Sandy Fitzwilliam, was credited with having an incredibly motivated staff who acted as if they owned the company. In fact, the article referred to Fitzwilliam as "the Empowering Manager."

Maybe I ought to talk to him, thought Michael. Most of the consultants I've met over the years have never actually managed anything themselves. Maybe I can talk with this Fitzwilliam guy in practical terms.

It seemed like a good idea, yet Michael was reluctant as he dialed information for Fitzwilliam's number. He always hated to admit he needed help. It drove his wife crazy that he would never stop to get directions when they were lost. He would drive around stubbornly trying to figure out how to get to their destination on his own. Only as a last resort would he stop and ask for help.

I guess this is one of those "last resort" times, Michael thought. My board is not going to wait forever while I figure out how to make this company profitable again.

With that thought as his motivation, Michael dialed the Empowering Manager's number. After two rings, he was greeted by a woman's voice saying, "Hello!"

"I'd like to speak with Sandy Fitzwilliam," Michael requested.

"Speaking," was the quick reply.

Michael was caught completely off guard. It never even entered his mind that Fitzwilliam could be a woman. Sandy Fitzwilliam broke the silence by asking, "Hello, are you still there?"

"Yes. Yes," stammered Michael.

"What can I do for you?" she asked politely.

Michael's mind was racing a mile a minute. Even though he was uncomfortable asking for help and desperately wanted to hang up, he found himself reluctantly explaining his situation and his need for some advice.

"We've streamlined our company so people can take more initiative and respond to customers more quickly. But people are still sending most decisions back up the hierarchical ladder. I've talked a lot about empowerment, and I can't understand why. . . ."

"Excuse me, Mr., uh. . . ."

"Oh, I'm sorry—my name is Michael Hobbs."

"Can you be more specific about what exactly is the problem?" the Empowering Manager continued.

Michael gulped and thought for a moment. Then he said simply, "People won't run with the ball."

"Let me ask you something," she began. "Have you ever arrived at a retail store one minute after closing time, only to find the door locked? You needed something badly, and you saw people inside, so you knocked on the door—and nobody even looked up."

"Yes. That happened to me just last week!" Michael exclaimed.

"Whose fault did you think it was? Who did you blame as you drove away?"

"The employees, of course!" Michael answered. "I bet the manager wasn't even there, and the workers were watching the clock, anxious to close shop. They probably weren't even thinking about me. They just wanted to get the heck out of there."

"Wrong!" Fitzwilliam chimed.

"What do you mean, wrong?" Michael asked defensively.

"Of course the employees were anxious to leave. But you're wrong about who was to blame. The fault was the owner's. Whoever the owner is, he or she did nothing to make the people who work there feel like they own the business. Otherwise, they would have opened the door."

Michael thought it over in silence.

"Let me ask you another question," the Empowering Manager went on. "If people were given the option, do you think they'd choose to be magnificent or ordinary at work?"

"Magnificent."

"Do you really believe that? Or are you just saying it because you think you should believe it?"

"Why would you ask that?" Michael inquired.

"Because I need to know about your real, honest-to-goodness, core beliefs. If you don't have a basic faith in people, it's time for us to hang up. Empowerment depends on a strong belief and trust in your people."

Michael was taken aback. Wow, he thought, this woman doesn't beat around the bush at all.

He answered reluctantly, "Well, if you must know, I don't have that much faith in people. It's partly because of the hierarchical thinking I grew up with and because this thinking has been reinforced in my MBA program and my work experience. When I think about it, it makes sense that people would rather do their best at their jobs, given the choice. But that's when I stop to think about it. My gut instinct is that people are not that responsible. They may like freedom to do what they want on the job, but they do not want to be held accountable when things go wrong."

"I appreciate your honesty," the Empowering Manager replied. "Recognizing that the world might pass you by if you don't change is half the battle. This is particularly true when you understand what empowerment is and what it is not."

"That would certainly help," said Michael. "I've never actually heard a good definition. To me it has always seemed that empowerment is giving people the power to make decisions, but somehow that just has not worked in our company."

"That's what a lot of people think, but true empowerment is *not* giving people power," she explained. "People already have plenty of power—in the wealth of their knowledge, experience, and motivation—to do their jobs magnificently. We define empowerment as 'letting this people power out and focusing it on company issues and outcomes.' But you see," she added in a more subdued tone, "I've learned this the hard way by making many mistakes along the road to empowerment.

"Real empowerment has at its core a sense of ownership," she continued. "And it starts with the belief system of top management. Too many leaders still need to get over the notion that their people head off to work every morning asking themselves how they can get by with doing as little as possible today."

"When you put it that way, it sounds terrible," said Michael. "Are there that many leaders who have so little trust?"

"I can only go by their behavior," said the Empowering Manager, "and by the results they get from their employees. It's not that people in organizations are unable to be their best—they're afraid to be their best. Most organizations are set up to catch people doing things wrong rather than to encourage and reward them for doing things right."

Michael thought about that. "You know," he said, "I agree. I've seen organizations like that." Then he paused, sunk deep into thought, and finally said, "That's part of the problem at my company." Again he paused, then added, "If we are to survive, our company has to be a place where people are proud to show what they can do and not afraid to be their best! I'm just not convinced that empowerment can get us there."

"I think your doubts are sincere," she said, "and I sense that your real satisfaction will come when you see people taking charge. I also pick up on your hunger for winning. You obviously don't want to settle for running an ordinary company. But I need to remind you that empowerment is a top-down, values-driven issue. That's why I had to check out your values. If you and your other managers cannot change, it will be hard to create a culture of empowerment for your people."

"So I passed, huh?" Michael said sheepishly.

"For now. Can you come by my office at 2 P.M. this coming Tuesday?"

Michael quickly glanced at his calendar and said, “Sure. I’ll see you on Tuesday.”

Just before she hung up, the Empowering Manager added, “We’ll see if we can get you and your company started down the road to the Land of Empowerment.”

Shortly before two o’clock the following Tuesday afternoon, Michael pulled his car into the parking lot at Sandy Fitzwilliam’s company and turned off the engine. From the passenger seat he picked up his electronic notebook and looked at the summary statement he had written there after his phone conversation with the Empowering Manager:

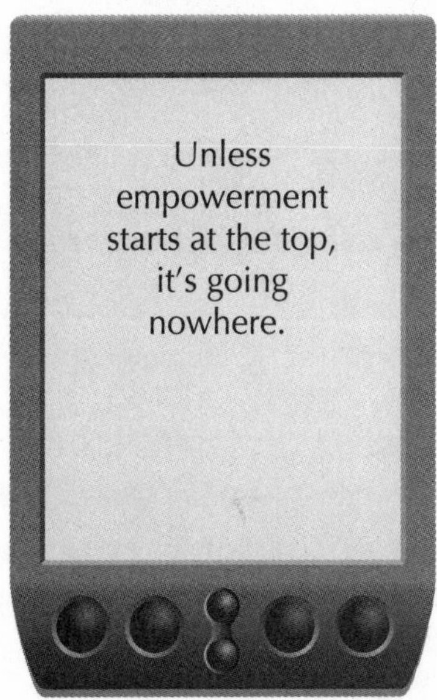

"**YOU CAN** go right in," smiled the woman at the desk outside Sandy Fitzwilliam's office.

Michael found the Empowering Manager standing by the window looking out. She turned and greeted him with a firm handshake. "I'm Sandy Fitzwilliam. Nice to meet you."

"Thank you for taking time to see me," Michael began.

"Don't get too excited until you find out whether or not I can help you. Do you recall what I said as we hung up last week?" Sandy asked seriously.

Michael thought for a minute. "Frankly, no."

"I told you that you were starting a journey."

"Oh, yes," said Michael. "Something about a journey to the Land of Empowerment. Sounds more like a ride at Disney World than anything else. I honestly don't know what you mean by it."

"It's not a fantasyland," she clarified. "It's real. What do you think it might mean?"

"Well," said Michael, letting his mind roam, "the word *journey* suggests that it might take some time to get there."

Sandy nodded.

Encouraged, Michael went on. "It also conjures up tales of adventure, where one follows roads that lead over steep mountains and through dark forests. Unexpected things happen. There are lots of tests along the way. Something like that."

"Very good," she nodded. "And, what about the phrase *Land of Empowerment*?"

"Sounds like a land different from the one where I'm living now, that's for sure—one where the customs of the inhabitants are not the ones I was raised with and have become accustomed to seeing. It's foreign."

"You've done well," Sandy said, smiling with obvious satisfaction. "Even though you resisted the concept at first, it feels like you've grasped the main ideas, the time it takes, and the degree of difficulty. I particularly like the fact that you think of the Land of Empowerment as being foreign. Most of us who try to empower others get in our own way because of our traditional thinking. We are modern and sophisticated in so many technological ways and yet traditional and naive in our beliefs about people and organizations."

"But come on, now—is it really that hard?" asked Michael.

Sandy just stared at him with no reply, so he added, "Well, there's my answer. I wouldn't have come here if I'd had an easy time of it. I was hoping you could just hand me a ready-made formula."

Sandy smiled. "I'd be doing you a disservice if I gave you a pep talk about empowering people, handed you a set of rules, and said, 'Go do it.' As you've already learned, you may want your people to take the initiative, but at first they may not be able to act empowered. This shouldn't be surprising. To use your analogy of a foreign land, they don't yet know the language or the customs of the Land of Empowerment."

Michael nodded as he began making some notes.

"And neither do you."

Michael looked up from his notes, and Sandy continued, "You and your managers may not yet be ready to deal with an empowered workforce. It means learning a whole new way to manage—managing project teams, cross-functional teams, and even self-managed teams rather than work groups.

"Remember what I told you on the phone: Empowerment is not giving people power—they already have it!"

As Michael nodded, Sandy pointed to a large plaque on her wall:

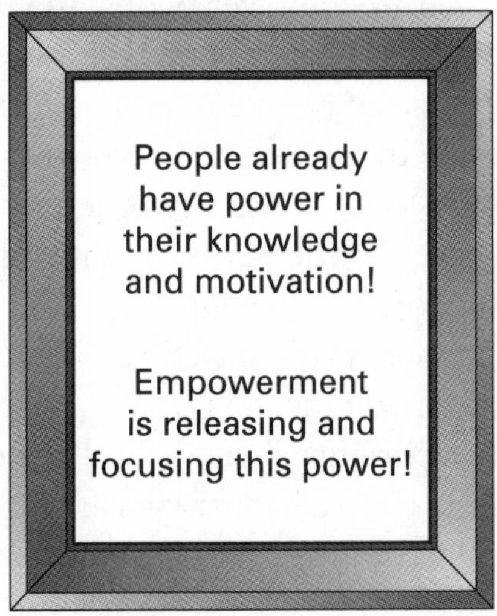

Michael's solemn look told her that he was mulling this over.

"Whatever happens, it's going to take time for you to get to the Land of Empowerment, and this journey is going to test you and others in your organization time and time again. You'll be impatient because of the lack of quick results, and you'll suffer setbacks.

"You or your associates will question why you ever started or whether the destination is worth it. The only thing that will keep you going is a huge amount of faith and trust in the journey and a genuine desire to create a better company for yourself and others."

She continued, "Have you ever tried to put into action something you believed deeply in, only to find out later that you'd been going about it all wrong?"

"Quite a few times," Michael admitted.

"You'll have that same experience with empowerment. In fact, you've come here because what you've tried to do so far to empower people in your organization hasn't worked. You reduced layers of management and authorized people to make more decisions, but now you see that is not real empowerment. So the question now is 'Are you willing to let go of what you still think is true about empowerment and about how organizations work?'"

Michael pondered the question. "Yes," he said, "if I understand what you mean."

"My own experience," Sandy said, "and that of others, suggests that this journey will be a series of discoveries. One of those discoveries may be that the path you have chosen won't get you there. The energy and intention you've already devoted to empowering people will have to be rechanneled."

"That's what you mean when you say that I have to have trust in the journey itself?" questioned Michael.

"Exactly."

"OK, I'm beginning to get it," said Michael. "I see that empowerment is not going to happen suddenly; I'm going to have to hang in there. But how will we know if we're making any progress along the way? My board will want to know that for sure."

"That's tricky, too. In the early stages, gains will be small. Yet it's important to keep an eye out for them and to celebrate every one. You see, the nature of success itself has changed. There used to be clear signposts, but in these times of constant change and threats to survival, managers can no longer count on the traditional benchmarks for success."

"Sounds like I'm going to have to convince my board that although it may be difficult to know we're getting there, it's not impossible to measure progress. We'll just have to find a new way to look for the signs," Michael ventured.

"That's exactly right," Sandy said. "And there are other, less obvious payoffs that are significant and long lasting. An example is the feeling of ownership that comes over people in an empowered culture. If you're open and receptive, even the times when you seem sidetracked will yield important findings. Also, right in the midst of all that frustration, you'll learn that you are being changed into an empowering person. It's as if the journey and the destination are one and the same."

"That sounds great on the surface, but I still have some serious reservations about the whole idea of empowerment," said Michael. "Being empowered as a manager isn't very exciting if you're wondering about what you will be doing once the work force becomes empowered. To be honest with you, my managers and I worry that empowering the workforce will lead not only to our loss of power and control but also to loss of our jobs."

Sandy nodded, acknowledging her appreciation for Michael's concern. "I understand that's a fear," she replied, "and it's a common one. When I first got into empowerment, I was also fearful of losing my job, at least the managerial job I thought I should do. I was afraid that if my people made all these decisions that I used to make as a manager, there would be too little managing left for me to do. Then I realized that you don't lose your job from empowering people; you just get a different one. Rather than directing, controlling, and supervising your people as in the past, you serve as a linking pin between your people and the rest of the organization. Your role actually becomes even more vital and engaging."

"What do you mean by linking pin?" puzzled Michael.

Sandy explained, "Your new role as an empowering manager is coordinating efforts, acquiring resources, strategic planning, working with customers, coaching people, and the like. Everything you do is to help your people be more effective in developing and using their talents and energy to achieve company goals. Now you work for them rather than them working for you."

The two leaders sat quietly deep in thought. This was obviously an important issue.

Finally, Sandy broke the silence. "Trust me. This new role will become clear to you as you learn more about empowerment."

"OK—for now," smiled Michael.

"Are you ready, then, to begin the journey to the Land of Empowerment?"

"As ready as I'll ever be," replied Michael. "Where do I start?"

Sandy pointed in the direction of her office door and said, "You have to start out there, with my colleagues in this organization."

"Your colleagues?" Michael repeated.

Sandy nodded. "The people I work with in this organization, no matter what position they may occupy, are my colleagues, my associates, my partners. If I create an environment that allows them to make this a great organization, they have the potential every day, through their every action, to make that happen. So they are the real source of the understanding you seek—not me." With that, she stood up and ushered Michael out the door.

Michael found himself standing outside the office, bewildered. He walked over to the woman who had shown him in. "I'm Michael Hobbs," he said.

"I know," smiled the woman.

"Are you Ms. Fitzwilliam's secretary?"

"Actually, I'm her colleague," came the reply.

Michael found himself thinking, how did I know she was going to say that?

Then the woman added, "My name is Amelia Engel. How may I help you?"

"I want to find out about how empowerment works around here. So I guess I'd like to talk to some of your, um, colleagues."

"We're all involved in making this an empowered organization," replied Amelia, "so anyone here could help you."

"Perhaps I should start at the bottom. That's where empowerment really has to go, isn't it?"

"Not really," smiled Amelia. "Anyone who interacts with our customers is considered to be at the top."

"OK, OK," laughed Michael. "Then maybe I should start at the top."

"Let me suggest that you talk to Robert Borders in our Billing Services Area," said Amelia, picking up the phone. "They've made tremendous progress in the last year by reducing billing errors by 37 percent and response time to customer billing inquiries by 50 percent. I'll see whether Robert is available."

THE FIRST KEY: SHARE ACCURATE INFORMATION WITH EVERYONE

A SHORT TIME later, Michael found his way to the billing response center that served the company's larger customers. Robert had suggested they meet there to get a firsthand look at the operation.

Michael was surprised that it appeared to be a fairly standard-looking operation, with the same kind of computers his own company used. The people even looked the same, except perhaps a little more engaged but also relaxed—almost like they were having fun. But at this point he didn't know what to expect, so he decided to just try to take it all in and learn. That was why he was there, after all.

A young man approached him. "Hi, I'm Robert Borders. You must be the executive Amelia called me about. What can I do for you?"

"I just finished talking with Sandy Fitzwilliam, and now I need to talk with some people in your company about empowerment. But even though empowering people is my goal, I'm skeptical. I've tried to institute empowerment with my company, and, frankly, I haven't seen much change. But I'm beginning to think we may have gone about it incorrectly—maybe I don't even know what real empowerment is, much less how to create a culture of empowerment."

"How long have you been at it?" Robert asked.

"Six months," said Michael.

Robert nodded. "All people have doubts at the beginning. But that shouldn't be surprising. They're being asked to buy into something on faith. Not only have they had little or any experience with being empowered; in many cases they've been unempowered. Also in the beginning they don't know how the process is going to work. They have no sense of WIIFM."

"What's WIIFM?"

"What's-In-It-For-Me. You can't blame people for being skeptical. Enough flavor-of-the-month programs have come and gone for people to believe that this is just another one of them. That was certainly the attitude here. And many of the younger members of the company have seen a big shift in the implicit contract between companies and their people—they have grown up with layoffs and have a built-in doubt of what company leaders say.

"In fact, when Sandy started telling us that her goal was to build an organization of colleagues where everybody's potential would be used, we thought it was just another line to get more work out of us, and for what reason, we thought."

"Hmm," Michael mused. "That could explain why people aren't acting empowered in my company.

Beliefs change slowly, especially when there's a cloud of doubt, huh?"

"It takes time. At first, we didn't believe Sandy knew what she was talking about. Even if she was sincere, we doubted it could work. But now, we know she was right," Robert added. "And it's not just that people feel better. We're much more effective and efficient than we were before. We feel better about ourselves, our leaders, and our company. We feel a real sense of ownership and empowerment."

"Well, talk is cheap," Michael said, impatiently. He was irritated by the obvious satisfaction Robert felt with his department. Then he asked, "How did you get where you are today? Something must have happened to release all that energy. It didn't just. . . ."

"Information," interrupted Robert, "accurate and timely information."

"Information?" Michael echoed. "But what kind? Don't people already have lots of information available through technology systems?"

"Of course they do," said Robert, "but what they need most is information about how the business is doing—profits, costs, budgets, market share, productivity, defects, and so on. You want to share accurate information that can be used for making good business decisions in a timely manner, the same information you as a manager use to make decisions."

Robert took a little card out of his shirt pocket and handed it to Michael:

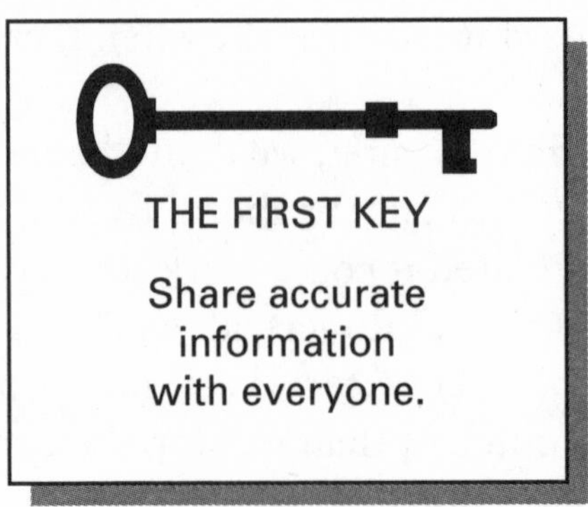

"I don't get it," said Michael. "Share detailed information about company performance throughout the organization? That sounds risky. What if the information paints a bad picture for the company? Wouldn't that lead to chaos or anarchy? I can't imagine doing that in my company. And further, I think that many others would be very uncomfortable doing it. Some information just cannot be shared with everyone."

"Then you can't create an empowered organization," replied Robert. He paused for emphasis and then said, "I'm going to tell you something. I know you're a CEO, a president and all, and perhaps if I didn't have Sandy as an example I'd hesitate to say this because of respect for your position. But that's the trouble right there—the perceived difference in people's positions that hangs over from the old hierarchical mind-set and assumptions. That perceived division between 'superior' and 'subordinate' is no longer very useful in business organizations. In fact, it works directly counter to success. Success today depends on team effort. And we have all the technology we need to engage people in the business. But our assumptions limit its use—it sure did here in the beginning." Robert paused.

Michael crossed his arms and stared at Robert. This conversation is just not very helpful, he thought. But after a few more moments of silence, he nodded for Robert to continue.

"You can walk out of here," said Robert slowly, never taking his eyes off Michael. "You can deny what I'm saying until you're blue in the face. But the fact remains that those leaders who are unwilling to share accurate and detailed performance information with their people will never have their people as partners in running the company successfully and will never have an empowered organization. This act of sharing information about the business and its markets is absolutely crucial to empowering people to act like entrepreneurs in an organization. That's why it's the first key."

"You're asking for a major shift in thinking—almost a lobotomy," said Michael with an uncomfortable laugh.

"I know it," said Robert. "Every leader has to fight the battle against habit and tradition in the depths of his or her own heart. Each leader has to make a leap of faith. The most crucial place the shift has to occur is inside you."

"It certainly would be a big first step for me," said Michael emphatically.

"And why wouldn't it be?" asked Robert. "You happen to be one of those managers who's caught in what we call the 'big left turn.'"

"What's the big left turn?" asked Michael.

"It's the huge, all-encompassing collapse of traditional boundaries that's taking place due to the sudden explosion of information. Information is bringing down walls all over the world. It's happening in all of our institutions at once, and it can be very scary.

"Communication barriers like the Iron Curtain, the Berlin Wall, and apartheid began to crumble long before anyone made the collapse official. Why? The flow of information could not be controlled any longer, no matter how hard anyone tried."

"And the explosive growth of Internet use during the 1990s has made the flow of information even more uncontrollable," Michael mused. "People have access to all sorts of information about their companies, as well as the markets and events that will shape the future in which the companies must operate."

"Right," Robert agreed. "People can obtain all kinds of information, so it is all the more important that we make available accurate and timely information about our companies. And it is hard for managers to take the risk to share so much information. They are afraid of violating HR or legal or stock exchange rules, and I believe they are afraid of losing control. Sharing all information, even sensitive information, takes courage. But don't wait around for it to feel good to you. Just take a leap of faith and *do it*. It'll feel good later on."

"Just do it," Michael repeated. "But what about privileged information?"

"What do you mean by 'privileged information'?" asked Robert.

"You know—guarded information; known to a few; only certain people can have it; it's sensitive," explained Michael.

"Let me ask you," said Robert, "how would you feel if you were one of the people on the 'outside' who was denied access to the privileged information, particularly when you knew the information was only a computer keystroke away?"

That caught Michael off guard. He hesitated for a moment and then smiled. "I'd feel pretty ticked off and left out, among other things. It would support any doubts I had about managers."

"I bet you would feel ticked off," laughed Robert. "Withholding information carries all kinds of messages. It makes people think, 'I'm not in the know. They don't trust me. They think I'd do bad things with the information if I knew it. They think I'm too dumb to understand it,' and so forth."

"People don't feel trusted," Michael reiterated. He was starting to understand the importance of sharing accurate and timely information.

Robert nodded. "On the other hand, there's no better way to show people that you trust them than to share sensitive information. Information about this company used to be private and unavailable to most of us. When Sandy began sharing performance information, like margins, profitability, costs of losing customers, and so forth, she sent a very strong signal to everyone that she trusted us; that she wanted us to use our knowledge and talents to help the business succeed."

"So you're saying that trust is crucial for an empowered organization."

Robert nodded enthusiastically. "And if people throughout the organization don't feel trusted, effective decision making grinds to a halt. People don't feel empowered, and therefore they don't act empowered. You see,

People without accurate information cannot act responsibly.

People with accurate information feel compelled to act responsibly.

"That's beginning to make sense to me," muttered Michael.

"It's the heart of the matter!" said Robert.

"People without accurate information cannot monitor themselves or make sound decisions. People with accurate information can and want to act."

Michael began thinking about his own organization. He realized that people at his company did not have the information to really understand the business and its performance results. Nor did they operate with a basic sense of trust. He was beginning to grasp the idea that sharing privileged information, like Sandy did with her colleagues, could help people be more responsible and also start them on the road to building a strong sense of trust.

As he was thinking, Michael suddenly got a blinding flash of the obvious. He scribbled something on his organizer screen and then looked Robert squarely in the eye. "Of course! What you're saying is that accurate business information is the currency for responsibility and trust in the Land of Empowerment."

Robert smiled and nodded. "Every leader wants responsible and trustworthy people in the organization. But stop and think: How do you go about developing responsible, trustworthy people? There's only one way."

"You trust them with complete and accurate information," Michael said.

"And that means action, not words or smiles," said Robert. "You've got to show you trust them by sharing all kinds of information—even sensitive information. Have you talked a lot about empowering people in your company?"

"We sure have—and with no results to show for it!"

"The same thing happened to us," said Robert. "When we began talking about empowerment several years ago, that's all it was—just talk. Nobody really believed anything would happen. We all felt it was just the latest fad, or worse just another management trick. One of my associates who has been around the company for many years said, 'Just wait—this too shall pass.'

"Sandy kept going around saying things like, 'You gotta believe that the magic happens where the workforce is.' But we didn't know if she and the other managers really meant it. It wasn't until she began to share information with everyone that we really started to believe. The sharing of what had once been confidential information about performance, profits, true market share, and such, made us realize that this was a safe place for us to think and use our real talents and knowledge."

Michael looked again at the card Robert had given him. "I'm beginning to see the real reason behind this first key. Information sharing to me was always purely functional—you know, linked to people's functions in the organization. So when you gave me this card, one of the reasons I resisted was not understanding why people needed more information to do their jobs. It seems with our computer systems that they already have lots of information—maybe sometimes so much that it overwhelms them. But now I realize that what they need is accurate, complete, and timely information about our company and its business performance measures. If they are to become responsible and to feel trusted, they need the same information I have and use!"

"That's it!" exclaimed Robert.

"But what about goals?" sighed Michael. "Throughout my career I've always understood that goal setting should be first. If information comes first, where do goals fit in?"

Robert smiled and said, "I was waiting for you to ask that, because everyone does. Goals are still very important."

"In most organizations goals are established at the top and then handed down. People feel no commitment to them because they haven't been involved in establishing them. I think you can sense how that wouldn't work in an empowered organization. To break down the traditional hierarchical belief that all the 'brains' are at the top of the organization, you have to start building trust first. Once information sharing takes place, and people have begun the journey together toward the Land of Empowerment, then goal setting takes on real meaning."

"So basically, you're telling me to wait and see," Michael said.

"That's right," Robert agreed. "Remember, information sharing is only the first step on the journey. I'd like to tell you more, but I've got to get back to an urgent project right now. Why don't you talk to some of my other colleagues about the additional keys to empowering people? Janet Wo over in Inventory Processing is someone I've worked with a lot. I happen to know that Janet has a meeting this afternoon, but let me call her and see if she'll meet with you tomorrow morning."

Robert set up a meeting for 8 A.M. the next day. Michael left the building, his mind racing with thoughts about the sharing of accurate, complete, and timely information. When he reached the parking lot he sat in his car for a while, summarizing in his electronic organizer what he had learned:

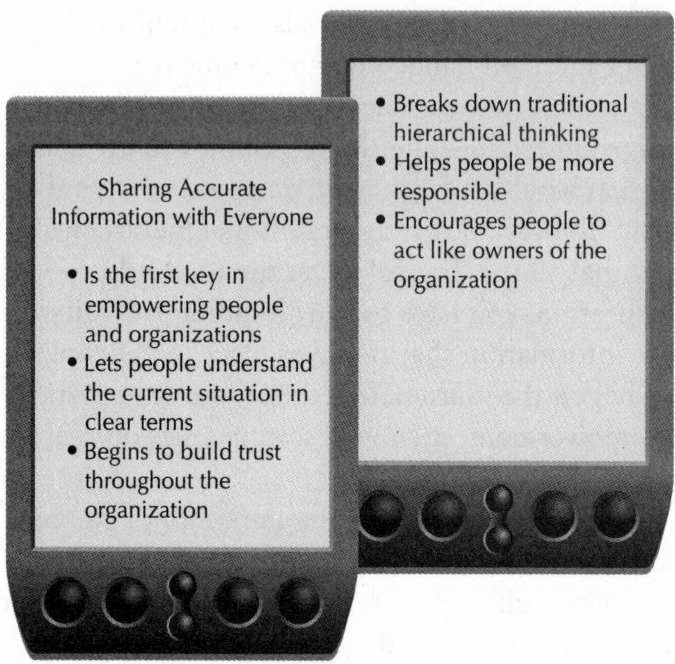

As he drove home, Michael thought about how the new things he had learned clashed with his former beliefs and attitudes. I wonder what the other keys are, he thought. And will they be as big a surprise as the first one was?

THE SECOND KEY: CREATE AUTONOMY THROUGH BOUNDARIES

THE NEXT morning Michael was back bright and early. As he entered the Inventory Processing Area, a woman approached him and introduced herself as Janet Wo.

"I understand you've been hanging out with some of my colleagues—Sandy Fitzwilliam and Robert Borders," said Janet. "This stuff about empowering people can be pretty confusing at first. Remembering how it was for me, I imagine your head is spinning."

"Well, you're right," said Michael. "I was surprised to learn how sharing information works to establish trust and help people improve their work processes. But I can't imagine that information alone can be enough. What comes next?"

"To answer that question, let me ask you to consider things from the viewpoint of management. In order for people to be empowered, do you think they need more structure or less?"

"Why, less structure, of course. To empower people, you want to free them up, not restrict them with rules."

"OK," Janet replied in a noncommittal way. "Now, think about where people are when you embark on the journey to the Land of Empowerment. They've heard about empowerment. Most of them probably want to be empowered. But what's their total experience of what it means to be empowered? Do they really understand what it means to be allowed to use their experience and knowledge but at the same time to be held fully accountable for the results, whether good or bad?"

"Probably not much. They probably like the freedom part, but the accountability part concerns them."

"That's right."

"I see," Michael mused. "They'd be lost, or at least a little confused. Maybe they would need structure after all."

"They would, but it's a different kind of structure. Usually we think of structure as a kind of boundary that limits what we can do. Here we are talking about boundaries that clarify the range within which people have autonomy," said Janet. With that, she handed Michael a small card that read:

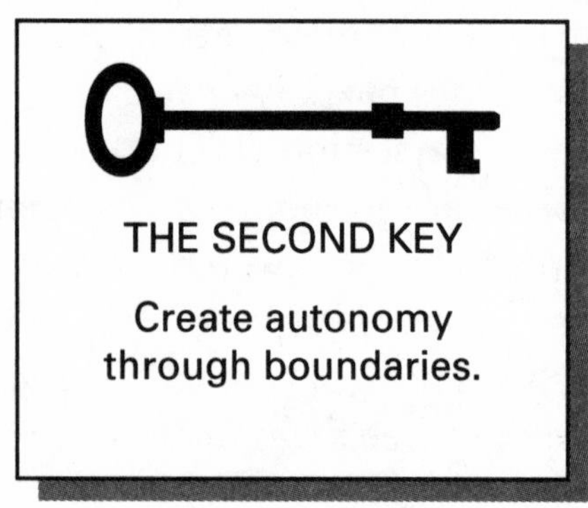

"People have to learn new ways of thinking and working together," Janet went on. "To use an analogy, in the old horse-and-buggy days people used to throw the reins over the horse's neck, and the horse would take them home. That worked because the horse knew the way, but people didn't do that when they were starting out on a new journey."

"What you're saying is that with a lack of guidelines, people revert back to their old unempowered habits—they head back home to the familiar," Michael ventured.

Janet nodded. "Yes. Boundaries have the capacity to channel energy in a certain direction. It's like a river—if you were to take away the banks, the river wouldn't be a river anymore. Its momentum and direction would be gone."

"I guess a river without banks would be a very big puddle," said Michael, laughing. "I see what you mean. You want people's energy to have direction and impact."

"Also, consider the security there is in having boundaries," added Janet. "How would you like to play tennis with just the net—there would be no lines to define a court. You wouldn't know how to keep score, what good performance was, or how to improve your game."

Michael thought for a few seconds and then said, "I asked Robert where goal setting fits in and he essentially told me to be patient. Aren't goals an important part of this boundary process?"

"Absolutely," said Janet. "But there are other kinds of boundaries besides goal setting." Janet walked over to her computer and printed out a single sheet of paper. "Here's a list of the critical areas where we started to create new boundaries," she said.

Boundary Areas
That Create Autonomy

1. **Purpose** — What business are you in?
2. **Values** — What are your operational guidelines?
3. **Image** — What is your picture of the future?
4. **Goals** — What, when, where, and how do you do what you do?
5. **Roles** — Who does what?
6. **Organizational Structure and Systems** — How do you support what you want to do?

"That looks like a lot of structure and boundaries to create," said Michael.

"It is," answered Janet, "but it need not all be done at the same time. In fact, it can't. It must be created as you need it. In our company it began with top management drafting a compelling vision of our company as an empowered organization."

"A compelling vision," echoed Michael.

"Yes," said Janet. "A compelling vision involves the first three boundary areas on our list. It emotionally and intellectually captivates the members of your organization and crystallizes their needs, desires, values, and beliefs. The way to create a compelling vision is to articulate a picture of the future, an *image*, that clarifies the *purpose* of your organization—what business you are in—and illuminates the guiding *values.* And while empowerment is a process that engages everyone in the company, the direction of the company needs to be defined clearly by the management team, and refined and understood by everyone in the company."

"Can you give me an example?" said Michael.

"Sure. Way back when Apple Computer was getting started, Steven Jobs envisioned everyone having and using a personal computer, which was quite a dream at that time. The *purpose* of the company was to build and make available affordable information systems—computers. The underlying *value* was to create access to an easy-to-use computer for everyone, not for just a few. The *image* of the end result was a personal computer on every desk and in every household. As his vision became clear, the means to achieve it also became clear, so Jobs developed a method to mass-produce high-quality personal computers. A compelling vision creates the big picture for your company."

"Thanks," responded Michael, "but let me ask you a question about your company and this vision process. Did everyone get involved in clarifying your vision, and if so, how did that work?"

"They sure did," smiled Janet. "Each person in every department worked with their colleagues and leaders to translate the company vision into roles and goals that had meaning for them personally. Such translation of vision takes effort, but it is essential for every team and every person to understand how they will contribute to achieving the company's vision. We call that defining the little picture so that it is consistent with the big-picture vision.

"I always think in analogies," Janet continued. "In this case, I think of a jigsaw puzzle. The organizational vision is the big picture you end up with when you complete the puzzle. The specific role each person has to play in achieving the vision is like one individual puzzle piece. Each piece of the puzzle has a small picture on it that contributes to the big picture. In terms of our organization, each role has its own little picture."

"When you put it that way, each person's little picture is pretty important," Michael said.

"Absolutely. It's a translation of the big picture into the specific actions that an associate performs. Those actions are directed toward goal accomplishment. For people to be effective, they must see both the big picture *and* their role in achieving that picture."

"Most organizations do goal setting," said Michael. "How is your process different in the context of empowerment?"

"Our goal-setting process focuses energy. Without clear goals people can waste energy."

"Waste energy?" wondered Michael.

"Yes," said Janet. "Have you ever had your employees list ten things they think you hold them accountable for?"

"Why would I do that?" replied Michael. "We tell them what's expected of them, and they all get annual performance reviews."

"You may have just diagnosed one of your biggest problems," said Janet. "Tell me, when people leave their performance review sessions with you, do they feel validated or surprised?"

Michael reflected on the last three reviews he'd completed. "Come to think of it, they act surprised. Two of my last three reviews involved disagreements. The people said they didn't know they were responsible for certain areas."

"Sounds like you'd find the *Top Ten Planner* helpful. Since there is often a difference between what people think they're supposed to be doing on a day-to-day basis and what their manager thinks they should be doing, I recommend that each of them make a list and compare the priority of things on the two lists. Let me give you an example of how this *Top Ten Planner* works.

"A couple who are friends of mine own a convenience store. They were constantly in a quandary as to why things they thought were important weren't getting done around the store. So they asked their assistant to list the ten things she thought she was accountable for. This is the list the assistant produced." Janet handed Michael a slip of paper:

1. Shrink (inventory loss)
2. Cash over or short on the register
3. Stock shelves
4. Clean rest rooms
5. Test gas tanks for water
6. Fresh coffee at all times
7. Clean parking lot
8. Organize back room
9. Rotate stock
10. Ordering

"My friends, the owners, made a list of the ten things they held the assistant accountable for. It looked like this." She gave him another slip of paper (see next page):

"When they compared lists, the problem became obvious. And as they told me about it they said, 'The fault turned out to be ours as managers. We tell people we'll hold them accountable for end results—such as sales, service, and so on. But the things we talk to

1. Sales volume
2. Profit
3. Customer perception
4. Quality of service
5. Cash management
6. Overall store appearance
7. Just-in-time inventory
8. Training employees
9. Protecting assets (maintenance)
10. Merchandise display

them about day-in and day-out—the things that stick in their minds—are routine tasks. We were sending mixed messages. The *Top Ten Planner* really helped us to see what we were doing and to appreciate the pain we were causing our assistant as a result.

"'We'd been telling her things like these:

- Shrink is too high.
- Why is the second shift twelve dollars short?

- There are holes in the shelf stock.
- The bathroom is a mess.
- Have you tested the gas tanks for water yet?
- You're out of coffee.
- Who had a party in the parking lot?
- Looks like you cleaned the stockroom with a hand grenade!
- Put the new product in the back.
- Your order is late.'

"You probably heard from Robert Borders that people without accurate information can't be responsible," Janet said. "Well, in addition, people will never be empowered if they're not sure what their goals and roles are. In this case, the fact that the assistant didn't make the connection between the tasks she was doing and goals for which she was accountable was the owners' fault.

"The owners' daily feedback to the assistant fed the wrong goals and created a different focus by the assistant than was desired. They should have been saying things like these:

- 'Let me help you figure out why sales are down.
- What can we do to increase sagging profits?
- Let's find out what our customers think about no coffee and dirty rest rooms.
- Our gas customers have an impact on the impulse buying that is an important part of this business. Let's make sure they never get water in their gas tanks.

- If our cash is continually over or short, customers are probably being ripped off.
- First impressions are important. What do you think of the parking lot this morning?
- If the stock room isn't organized, we may have to tell a customer we're out of stock simply because we can't find a product.
- What employee training have you conducted this week?
- What is your schedule for rotating the displays so customers see different products?'"

"The difference is what we talk to people about and the way we talk to them," said Michael. "It's more like being a partner than being told what to do. I think that if I were the assistant and heard these kinds of messages consistently, I'd have more of a business perspective and feel more ownership."

"We've learned a lot from that story in our company," said Janet. "We've found that without clear goals that are consistently checked, people can't perform well or be empowered. In fact, highly skilled, creative people will waste a lot of time on less important activities, all the while believing they are doing what is expected of them. In the convenience store example, that might have meant that customers were waiting while someone swept the parking lot."

"I think I've got it," said Michael. "The connection between boundaries and autonomy is getting clearer. I've tried to summarize it in a way that makes sense to me." Michael showed Janet his organizer screen:

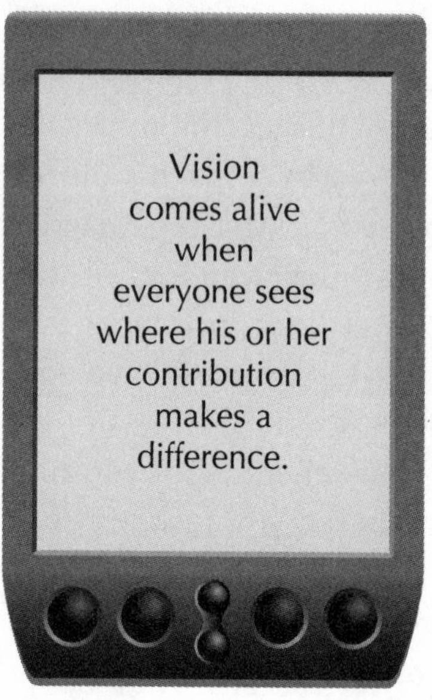

Janet chuckled and said, "Robert told me to watch out for you."

"What do you mean?"

"He said that while you might be resistant at first, once you grasp an idea, it doesn't take you long to run with it."

"Yeah, I guess so. I've always been an action person. I tend to grasp things quickly, and then I'm ready to get moving toward implementation. You've helped me understand vision and goal setting fit together, but tell me a little more about how values work to create autonomy," said Michael.

"Values are a key element of a compelling vision," said Janet. "As we began our journey toward the Land of Empowerment, we found we had to clarify our fundamental beliefs and then translate them into commonly agreed-upon values. The beliefs support the vision, the values makes it a reality by guiding our actions. You see, organizations don't really have values until the associates who work there verify the statements of belief as the way to operate. So Sandy involved us in a collaborative process of validating our values."

"How did she do that?"

"First she gave us a talk on values. She explained what values are and how they should guide our autonomous actions in working toward the vision of the company. Everybody around here remembers that talk like it was yesterday. People refer to it as her 'I Have a Dream' speech."

"What did she say?"

"*What* she said was pretty important, but the way she said it was what really got our attention. It was like she was consulting with us. You can't listen to her long without hearing her commitment to certain values. She spelled these out for us, but in such a way that it was obvious that they would work."

"She made us feel important—just like she did when she gave us all that privileged information. Except this time it wasn't, 'I can't believe she's telling us this!' It was, 'I can't believe she's asking us about this!'"

"You mean you felt really involved," Michael said with a smile.

"Yes. When somebody trusts you like that and asks for your involvement in defining and clarifying our values, you say to yourself, 'Why would I work anywhere else?' That speech was only the beginning, though. It was the validation process that followed that eventually got us all aligned with the same values."

"You mean you had an actual method of finding agreement on values?" Michael asked.

"Everyone supported the values that Sandy articulated. The agreement was more about the rules surrounding those values," answered Janet. "In our work groups we were given a series of directions for creating departmental dialogues. We discussed the values and the ways they would be acted out in our work."

"How did the meetings go?"

"There were some real surprises at first."

"How so?"

"We didn't know that we had been operating under differing assumptions until we were involved in the process. As we tried to agree on ways we would operate and treat each other, we kept getting blocked. Once we started discussing the values and listening to each other, as the directions told us to do, our eyes were opened. Defining what was meant by certain key value words became the most important part of the exercise.

"Again and again," continued Janet, "I heard people say, 'I never dreamed you looked at it that way!' One of the guys in my unit said that when we started out, we were like a bunch of iron filings, all spread out and pointing in different directions. The validating process was like a magnet passing over us, leaving us all aligned in unison."

"But that must have taken a lot of work time," Michael said.

"As managers, we thought so, too," Janet replied. "We were asking, 'Why are we doing all this stuff, when we need to be filling orders and making money?' But you know what? That process eventually saved us time! It was amazing!"

"How do you mean?"

"Ever since the values process, decision making has been much faster and easier. We have a shared set of values to guide us."

"I've just made another discovery about my own organization," Michael said. "We've been trying to get one simple statement across to everybody: 'If you see a problem, fix it.' Now I know why it's been so hard getting people to live by that statement."

"Oh?"

"The way we went about it was doubly wrong. First, people didn't choose the rule—it was imposed on them. Second, we had no process for listening to each other and reaching agreement, like your process for validating values. For all I know, there are as many interpretations of what that statement means as there are people in the company!"

"Without agreement on a rule, you can't focus energy on your purpose. Values serve as the driving force for purpose. All parts of your compelling vision have to be integrated," said Janet.

"Tell me how structure and systems fit in," asked Michael.

"Your vision tells you the right things to do, while your structure and systems, together with defined roles and goals, ensure that things are done right. Let me show you a graphic of how all these elements work together to create the boundaries that drive autonomy, and I might add, responsibility. Janet pointed to a framed picture she had hanging on the wall outside her office.

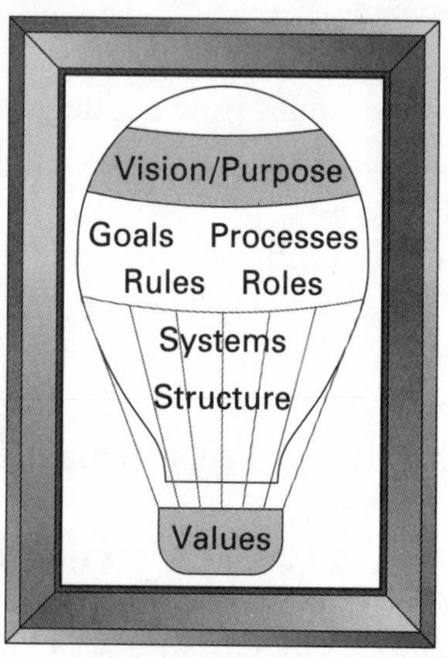

"And allow me to give you an example of what happens when some of these elements are not aligned," said Janet. "We wanted to coordinate our inventory activities with our sales process, so we suggested to the sales teams that we needed to improve planning. They were sympathetic, but when it came right down to it they wouldn't make the necessary changes in implementing the planning. Want to know why?"

"Sure."

"Their bonus was calculated on a formula that counted 'planning time' as 'nonproductive.' Planning time reduced their bonus! Once we changed the reward structure, the problem went away."

"So, organizational structures and systems that are already in place may hinder the process of empowering people to improve?"

"Right," said Janet. "But remember, these policies were created to support a control-oriented organization, not an empowered one."

Michael thought about that. Then he said, "My company has some policies that would inhibit people from being empowered. One is the requirement of a sign-off for purchases over certain amounts. Another is the demand for formal proposals on any changes that affect more than one department. The list goes on and on."

"Fortunately," assured Janet, "you can deal with each one as you go along. We found that the trust created by shared information made people feel free to express themselves about what was getting in the way of being empowered."

"Right there," said Michael, "might be another reason for using the first key—sharing accurate information—to start the process. It creates the basis of trust for the other steps. How did people express themselves, once they felt free to do so?"

"The question we heard most often was, 'Why do we do things this way?' Sandy encouraged it. Before long, everyone seemed to be examining every rule and policy and system to make sure it contributed to creating an empowered organization. In many cases the existing rules did contribute to empowering people. But a lot of other things went out the window. The whole organization took on a leaner, more streamlined feel.

There were other important questions, like What is my new role? What do I get to decide? How will I be held accountable? What are the new rules? How do I get some training on my new role?"

"All those questions must make for lots of uncertainty," said Michael.

"Actually, questions are the result of uncertainty," Janet smiled. "Change is always fraught with uncertainty. But in an information-sharing environment, where people operate with trust, uncertainty is something you can handle by communicating, getting agreement, and taking action. Such questions are a way of asking for clarification about the new boundaries."

"You know," said Michael, "I get a feeling you people here are in it for the long haul."

"Yes, it's a journey. We don't have to do it all at once! I notice you've been writing lots of notes in your organizer. May I see what you've written?"

"Sure," replied Michael. He showed Janet the screen on his organizer (see next page):

"Hey, that's great. You've got it," said Janet.

"Yeah, but I feel there must be more to it. Something is still missing," said Michael. "Information sharing, clarifying boundaries—what else?"

"To learn about the third key for the journey to the Land of Empowerment I suggest that you talk to Billy Abrams in Customer Service.

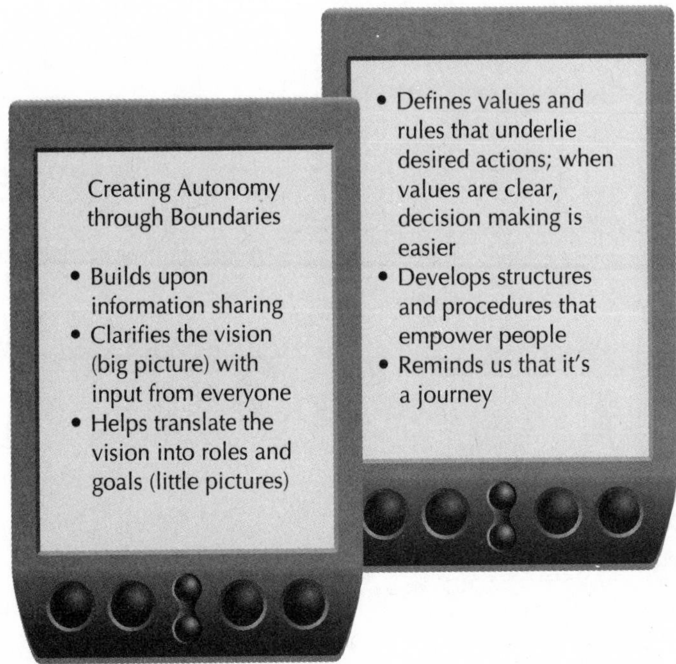

"Good luck to you on your journey, Michael," Janet said. "I'd like to leave you with something Sandy said that has always appealed to me: 'Empowerment isn't magic—just some simple ideas and a lot of smart work.'"

As Michael headed over to meet Billy Abrams, he was thinking, Simple ideas and a lot of smart work. That's what I want for my company.

THE THIRD KEY: REPLACE HIERARCHICAL THINKING WITH SELF-MANAGED TEAMS

MICHAEL SAW Billy Abrams hurrying toward him as he entered the Customer Service work area. Right away he sensed Billy was a high-energy person like himself—not much on talk and a pragmatist when it came to ideas.

As Billy led Michael through the work area, Michael said, "I sense you're a busy man, and I want to thank you for taking the time to meet with me. As you may know, I'm here to learn the third key to empowerment."

"No problem," said Billy, as if dismissing his last statement. "Tell me, did your company recently go through downsizing?"

"Yes, we did," answered Michael. "It's tough being responsible for eliminating jobs."

"I know what you mean. The same thing happened in this company."

"But in retrospect, it was absolutely necessary," Michael quickly added, "to survive and thrive as an organization. To be responsive to customers, we needed a company with as few management layers as possible.

But I realize now that while downsizing may create a need for empowerment, it is not anything like empowerment at all. And empowerment is certainly a lot more than authorizing people to make more decisions, which is what I used to think."

Billy and Michael strolled through groups of industrious people. A couple of associates were talking excitedly together in front of a computer screen. They looked up, smiled enthusiastically, and then went back to their task, as Billy and Michael walked by.

"Let me ask you something," Billy said. "When you finish flattening an organization by eliminating jobs, outsourcing services, and cutting out middle layers of management, what kind of a situation are you left with?"

"Well . . . ," Michael said slowly. He started counting on the fingers of one hand. "You've got upper management closer to where the action is. You've got supervisors with a wider span of control. And you've got resentful people who have been trained to carry out decisions made by others with 'privileged information' who they no longer trust."

"Exactly," said Billy. "All you're describing is a smaller bureaucracy with fewer layers and more negative attitudes. Decision making is still moving up the hierarchy. If we want an empowered organization, all that has to change. So the burning question becomes, What's going to take the place of the old hierarchy in terms of decision making?"

Michael began, "It seems like it would be everyone's responsibility now. But you can't just have an organization of autonomous people acting in isolation from each other. Maybe we need to depend on people working together in teams. People in teams can build off each other's specialized skills and knowledge. Yes, I'd vote for teams."

Billy nodded. They had been standing in the midst of a bustling stream of people. Billy led the way over to a couple of chairs at a table on the edge of the work area. Then he handed Michael a small card, the third one Michael had received:

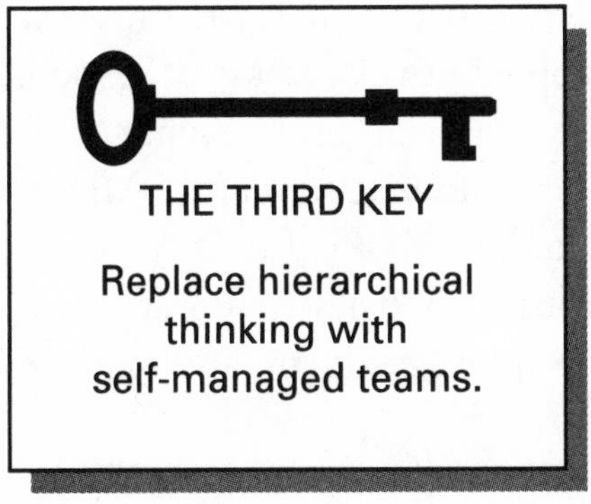

"Replace is a harsh word. I don't know how you can do that!" exclaimed Michael.

Billy responded, "Before the change, we'd had participative management and work teams. But they had always been in the context of the traditional hierarchy—mostly one-way communication, with decisions being handed down the line from the top. At best, the teams made recommendations; the managers made the decisions."

"But we realized we were faced with new competition. In our leaner organization we had to stay close and responsive to the customer yet still maintain internal controls that would protect our financial interests. The old hierarchy, and especially the accompanying hierarchical thinking, was too slow and cumbersome to accomplish that. And, as you implied, a team of empowered people is far more powerful than a disconnected set of individuals. So the solution was to get teams to do much of what the management hierarchy had done in the past. Our people had to learn to work in self-directed teams and to make and implement their decisions. Even at the lowest level, people began to grapple with the kinds of responsibilities that had always before been left to managers."

"What's a self-managed team?" Michael asked.

"It's a unique kind of team. It consists of a group of employees with responsibility for an entire process or product. They plan, perform, and manage the work from start to finish."

"Does the team have a manager?"

"There may be a manager on a team," explained Billy. "But, if it's a high-performing, self-managed, empowered team, you'd never be able to pick that person out. Everyone shares equally in the responsibilities. They might rotate team leadership, but the group would decide how."

"That must have been quite a change!" exclaimed Michael.

"It happened right here," said Billy as he looked around. "The people you see in this department have become part of high-performing, self-managed teams."

"You say that very proudly," Michael said.

"The mission of our department is an important one," Billy said. "We're really the sensing arm of the organization and the problem-solving arm for the customer. We're concerned with anything that goes wrong in the company's effort to serve customers, both external and internal customers. When an error occurs, we immediately gather all the information about it. Then we feed that information to our inventory and billing operations so that they understand what's been done wrong and can correct it for the future."

"Sounds like a big responsibility," said Michael.

"It is," agreed Billy. "On the other hand, it's not too large when viewed as a team effort. No one person has to do it alone. In fact, we who are on customer service teams can't even do it by ourselves. It's the whole organization's responsibility to provide good customer service. Our teams just lead the effort. The point you need to realize is that as teams we are constantly functioning the way only managers did in the past—assessing information from all over the company, analyzing that information, deciding what to do about it, and relaying our decisions to others."

"Hmm," said Michael. "I can see that people aren't sitting around waiting to be told what to do next. I've been watching your associates as we've been talking. They obviously count on each other, but everybody acts like a manager. In a hierarchical operation, people just do their assigned jobs; they don't go out of their way to help someone else. But here, everyone who comes by looks at me and smiles. I can sense their high energy and enthusiasm. They act committed—like it's their company."

"Right, but you've got to realize that it hasn't always been that way," said Billy, smiling. "In the beginning, my colleagues and I were—well, let's just say we were not immediately committed to this team idea. Many of us thought the idea of being a self-managed team sounded good, but we had no experience or understanding of how it would work."

"That's where the people are in my company," Michael said. "I have all these wonderful ideas from the past two days to bring to them about empowerment and building self-managed teams, but they probably haven't a clue about how to begin to operate in this new way.

Michael paused and then added, "It's like wanting something to function freely by itself, but in order for it to do that you have to give it a push."

"That's a very good way of talking about the paradox you experience in the beginning, before people are empowered," Billy remarked. "You can't just stand around hoping they'll take over. You have to start by giving them what they need at the place where they are. In our case, the managers had to begin with a rather directive style of leadership. They had to tell and show people how to begin acting more empowered."

"I've been getting that message," said Michael. "It seems that moving to autonomy begins with the need for boundaries and direction."

"Right," said Billy. "Guidelines and structure are essential in the beginning of the empowerment journey. People think directive behavior is telling people *how* to do their jobs, but our managers put the emphasis on telling us how to *manage* our jobs.

"It was exciting to suddenly be charged with using all the job knowledge we'd accumulated as a group. Almost everyone had ideas about how we could improve our service and responsiveness to our customers. But we didn't know how to make decisions as a team. We lacked team skills—skills for solving problems, managing meetings, managing the team, and handling conflict."

"So your managers focused their directive leadership not on telling you what to do but on developing the skills that were going to enable you to function on your own as a team."

"Right."

Michael had been summarizing in his organizer again. He showed Billy what he had written:

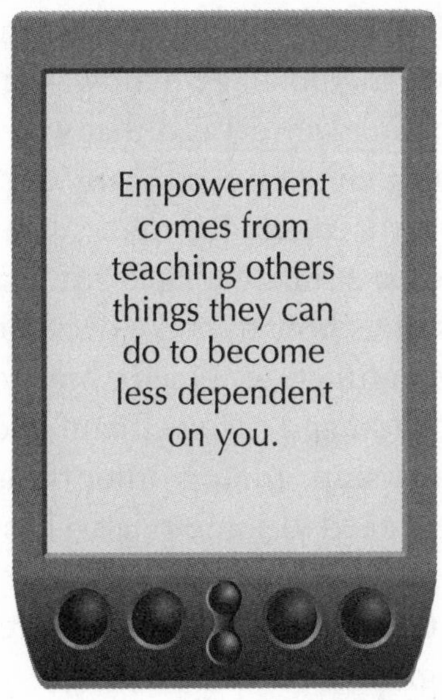

"That beautifully captures the idea for the starting point in training teams," responded Billy. "It was a lesson managers throughout our company had to learn the hard way.

"In the beginning, they thought the idea was to leave self-managed teams alone. So they abdicated their roles as coaches and then wondered why teams floundered. Everyone on our team was excited at first. But that lasted only for about a week. Then came denial—nobody wanted to admit we were totally confused. We did not want to recognize the widespread dissatisfaction."

"So what happened?" asked Michael. "Obviously things got straightened out."

"What happened was that Sandy recognized the state of chaos we were in. She called us all together to help diagnose the trouble. She took the blame for the confusion and never pointed a finger at anyone else. That showed us that management was on our side.

"In the meeting we realized that we wanted to be empowered but that we lacked many of the necessary skills. Together we concluded that we needed training in how to become a self-managed team. We needed training to teach us how to make decisions as a team, how to resolve conflicts as a team, how to monitor group participation and involvement, and how to share team leadership, among other things. We also realized that we needed some relatively strong leadership to guide and direct us as we worked to become self-managed teams. And we needed careful monitoring of our progress."

"In effect, you were asking managers to direct you," said Michael. "And it sounds like your managers began with a strong directive style, which is still confusing, given that the goal was to become empowered. I assume that to become empowered, sooner or later they had to stop using that style with you. Remember, you said when you become a high-performing team, you can't tell who the leader is. How did the team get away from the need for the directive leadership?"

"Slowly. Gradually. Almost imperceptibly at first," responded Billy. "Then faster. We began to hear stories of people and teams acting in empowered ways. Teams began to do things that only managers had done in the past, and do them better. Our managers began to act like facilitators and coaches. Some of them started to be masters at choosing just the right moment to do what we call 'standing there.'"

"What's that?"

"It's actually a critical skill of managing to empower. You have to know when to follow the rule":

Don't just do something— stand there.

"You mean knowing when not to step in so that somebody else can act?" asked Michael.

"Yes. The managers became adept at gradually transferring more and more responsibilities to the teams. The managers' fears dissipated as they found they were not losing control and that there was still plenty for them to do. They became more involved in strategic planning, working more with customers, looking at new equipment and procedures, researching and delivering the kind of training people will need in the future, as well as special company projects that had been on the back burner."

"There seems to be a delicate balance to this matter of transferring," Michael ventured.

"It's a dance," said Billy. "Like dancing, though, once you get the hang of it, you trust your intuition. In empowering people and teams, you learn new ways of assessing people. The best part is watching employees become associates. It's a lot of fun to 'lead' them occasionally to just a little bit more responsibility than they think they can handle. Then when it turns out you were right and they do handle it, it's great to see the pride in their faces!"

Michael paused, thought for a moment, and said, "You know, this team thing—correction, this empowered-team thing—can really be powerful. It's like a basketball team or a volleyball team that plays really well together. The team members' skills are transferable but also unique. They are given a chance to utilize their abilities and to continue to grow and develop. As individuals, they have the chance to become all that they can be and, at the same time, they're helping the organization become all that it can possibly be."

"It sounds like you've got it," said Billy.

"Yeah, maybe," said Michael, "but to make sure, why don't you take a look at this?" He handed his organizer over to Billy:

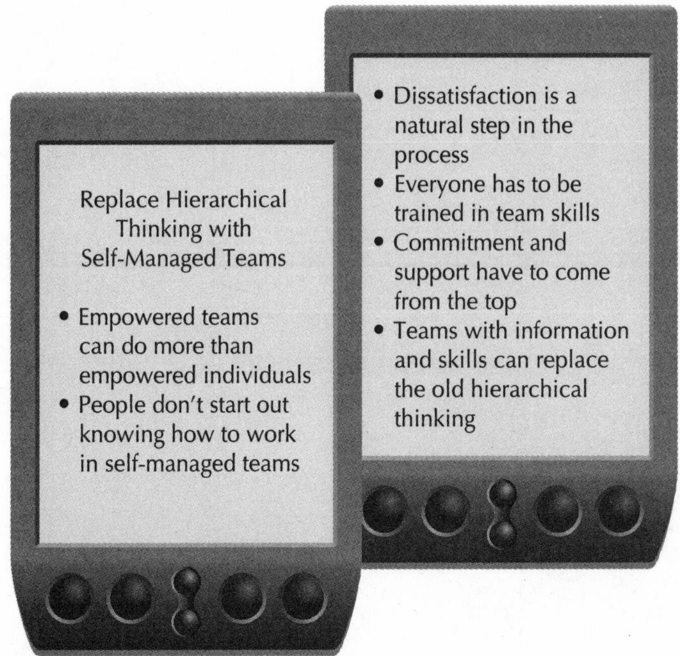

"You're right on the money," said Billy with a smile.

"You're a good teacher," insisted Michael.

After Michael thanked Billy, he headed home. As he drove, Michael could not stop thinking about what he had learned. One burning question that he wished he could answer kept coming to the surface. Finally, it got to him. He picked up the car phone and dialed Sandy Fitzwilliam's number.

"I wondered when I would hear from you again," she said.

"May I come by to talk with you right now?" Michael asked.

"Of course. I'll be waiting."

THE THREE KEYS IN DYNAMIC INTERACTION

AS MICHAEL walked into Sandy's office, he found her in a familiar pose, staring out the window. As she turned to greet him, he jumped right into his question, "So far, I've learned three keys to empowerment. They sound good, but do they work? Do they make a difference in performance or results?"

She responded, "Slow down a minute, and tell me what you've learned."

"OK. I've learned that there are three keys to empowerment that are part of a process for releasing the potential that is within people."

Michael showed her his summary notes (see next page):

After Sandy read his notes, Michael started talking excitedly again, continually referring to his cards and notes. For twenty minutes, he talked without letting her say a word. She sat back in her chair and listened intently.

When Michael finished, he was a bit out of breath. He looked at the Empowering Manager and waited

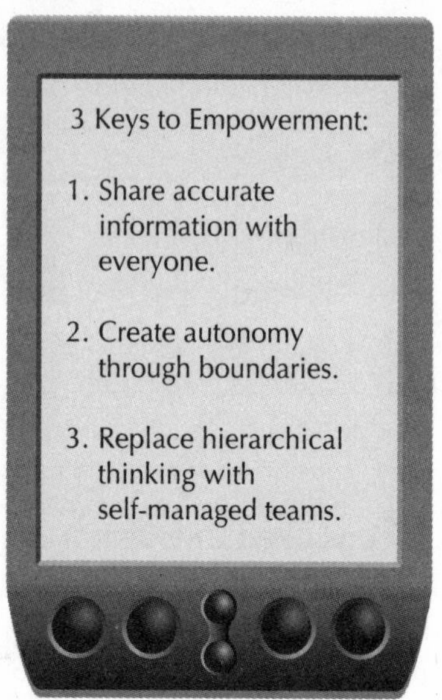

for her to say something. Finally she spoke. "It's evident to me that you understand the steps for creating an empowered organization. You get an A for your solid grasp of the main ideas."

"But can these three keys really lead to empowerment?" Michael asked. He had always been a bottom-line manager. "Isn't there more? Do they really improve performance and employee satisfaction?"

"Yes, yes, and yes," she replied with a smile. "Let me point out a few things regarding performance. This company has far exceeded even my expectations as we moved to empowerment. Now don't misunderstand; we were the leader in our geographic area even before empowerment, but we felt we could do better. And were we ever right!"

"Since we began the empowerment process," she continued, "our quality of customer service has exceeded 99.99 percent, while our revenue has gone up 10 percent a year and our costs have been cut 10 to 15 percent every year.

"On top of that, our people come to work excited every day; they find the increased responsibility very rewarding. And, they continue to come up with new ways to get work done faster, at lower cost, and with higher quality. They help us sense how the market is changing, and you wouldn't believe the many creative ways they help the company keep improving and innovating. Our business is booming, and our customers love us."

"I'm impressed," said Michael. "Tell me more about the performance and satisfaction that results from applying each of the three keys to empowerment."

"Once again I think you'd be better off talking to my colleagues," Sandy insisted. She picked up the phone and called Elizabeth Meadows in Fulfillment and found that Michael could see her the next morning.

"Elizabeth has some great ideas," she said. "She's right there on the front line, and I think you'll find that she's a results-oriented manager who can give you some more insights, particularly about the impact of sharing information and creating boundaries."

"That would be helpful," said Michael. "Do you have any final thoughts before I head off?"

"Three," Sandy replied. "First, as you may already have found, the three keys to empowerment are simple and easy to understand, but they are difficult to put into everyday action. Second, the process of moving people and the organization to empowerment is challenging and at times frustrating—you will want to give up many times before you get there. And, third, the three keys need to be viewed as operating in dynamic interaction with each other. While information sharing is the critical first step, empowering people takes all three keys, with a constant shifting in emphasis as needed."

Michael nodded, thinking, *All three in dynamic interaction.* Then he replied, "Thanks, that helps. I'm looking forward to meeting with Elizabeth Meadows."

GIVE EVERYONE THE INFORMATION TO ACT

MICHAEL ARRIVED early the next morning, hoping that Elizabeth could show him more about how empowerment worked and that it really gets results.

As he reached the Fulfillment Area, Michael was greeted by a tall, energetic woman. "Hi. I'm Elizabeth Meadows, and this is the area my associates and I own."

"What do you mean, you own it?" Michael asked.

"I mean," smiled Elizabeth, "we have all the information we need to make any important decision that has to be made to serve our customers, ensure quality of the products we sell, and make a profit for our company."

"Maybe that explains what happened when I was walking down here to meet you this morning," Michael said. "I overheard one of the fulfillment people telling someone on the phone that the missing items would be replaced at no cost and sent overnight to arrive tomorrow. Frankly, I was amazed. People in fulfillment don't usually have the authority to make that kind of decision."

Elizabeth, who had been peering at Michael as she listened, said, "Right. But people in fulfillment who have information can take on the responsibility for that kind of decision and know that it won't hurt the company. In fact, with information they would know just what dividends such excellent customer service will pay in the future. They can weigh the cost against the benefit of replacing the item at no cost."

"How can they know that?" asked Michael.

Elizabeth gestured to indicate the area around them. "Information!" she said with a smile. "Timely and accurate information that they can access freely."

For the first time, Michael really took in the graphs and charts that were everywhere on the walls, the computer screens filled with charts and tables of data, and the people working quickly and with little or no supervision.

"It's impressive, all right," Michael said hesitantly. "But I'm still skeptical about whether information sharing really works. As a matter of fact, that's why I came back to talk to Sandy Fitzwilliam. I need to know that the three keys to empowerment really work. I want results."

Elizabeth stared into Michael's eyes. Then she asked, "Have you ever noticed what happens when you occasionally see someone who wants to write a check to pay for groceries at the supermarket? The cashier verifies the person's ID and writes the number on the check, right? Then what happens?"

"The customer has to wait around while the cashier calls the manager or assistant manager to come over and approve the check," answered Michael. "The manager's talking to someone two aisles over as he or she is initialing the check. Now that I think about it, it doesn't seem right—especially since the 'wake-up call' you have given me."

"Why isn't it right?" asked Elizabeth.

"It sends a message that the store doesn't trust the cashiers and that the only employees there who have brains are the managers. The rest of the people might as well leave their brains at home because maybe they'll need them after work. Furthermore, it makes the customer feel distrusted, as well."

"Right," said Elizabeth. "In that process, what do you suppose happens to the cashier's self-esteem?"

"It's eroded, and that drop in esteem can easily rub off on the customer service."

"Right again. Now, what do you think would happen if the cashiers were given all the detailed information about the impact that bad checks have on the business and then were given check approval power?"

"Fewer bounced checks?" Michael wondered aloud.

"Right! That's what all the research says about places where it's been done. Further, the people have higher self-esteem and can provide more attentive customer service. When you give people information and a chance to act like owners, they'll usually come through," Elizabeth explained.

"That example is helpful, but can you give me another example?" Michael requested.

"Sure," said Elizabeth. "A friend of mine owns a restaurant. I was telling her about the power of sharing information with her people. She just wasn't buying it. She didn't think certain information was any of her people's business. To help her move from her 'stuck' position, I had her call together all the folks who work at her restaurant one night at closing time—the hostess, waiters, dish washers, chef, everyone. They sat at tables in small groups and answered the following question: 'Of every sales dollar that comes into this restaurant, how many cents do you think go to the bottom line as profit that can be returned to the owner or reinvested in the business?'"

"What did they say?" Michael asked.

"The lowest guess was forty-five cents and the highest was seventy-five cents. When my friend told them the correct answer was eight cents, they were shocked. They thought the restaurant was a money machine. Imagine what that misconception did to their attitude toward things like breakage and food wastage."

"They wouldn't care," said Michael.

"That's for sure," replied Elizabeth. "What really convinced my friend I was right about the power of sharing information was the remark the head chef made: 'You mean if I burn a six-dollar steak that we charge the customer fifteen dollars for, we have to sell at least five steaks to recover the six-dollar loss?' He had it figured out, and so did everyone else."

"Interesting," mused Michael. "So they started thinking in business terms. Did it make any difference?"

"Last year my friend declared, 'None of you will get a raise unless you can read our balance sheet and explain what it means.' And for the first time the restaurant showed over a 10 percent profit. When my friend shared 25 percent of that new profit with her staff, they were thrilled and started talking about additional ways they could cut costs and increase profits in the future."

"So you have to *show* people that you trust them by sharing information," commented Michael.

Elizabeth made another sweeping gesture toward the department and said, "As I said before, this place belongs to us. We own it! Now you can understand what our banner means," she said, pointing to a banner on the wall:

Give people the information to act;
then look for magic to happen!

"Fascinating," said Michael. "Tell me more about how has this worked for you?"

"We've learned that once you share information and trust starts to develop, you can begin to establish high standards," said Elizabeth. "You can talk about closing the gaps between what's happening today in terms of cost, profits, and so on, and what's possible tomorrow, and it makes sense to everyone. We usually try to identify a few particular measures—things like order-processing time, customer reactions to service, order fulfillment costs, for example—and then we share timely and accurate information about how we are doing. In fact, people can get the information when they need it so they can solve problems and recognize progress."

"Sounds like the old idea of continuous improvement," Michael interjected.

"It is," replied Elizabeth, "but, more importantly, it's also continuous innovation. Continuous improvement only makes sense when people have information and are trusted to use their skills and abilities. Continuous innovation goes even further. See that?" Elizabeth pointed to a sign:

> Every "misteak"
> is an opportunity
> to increase
> competence.

"Sandy had these signs posted around the company when we began our journey. Everyone thought she was crazy. Why would she want to encourage people making mistakes? The way you're looking at me, I'd say you think so, too."

"It bothers me," Michael said. "I'm a stickler for details, so I want to correct the spelling on your sign. More importantly, I don't want mistakes made in our organization. What does making mistakes have to do with improving performance?"

"Let me ask you something," said Elizabeth. "When a mistake is made in your organization, what's the first question asked: 'What can we learn?' or 'Who is to blame?'"

Michael answered, "I have to admit that most times it's 'Who is to blame?'"

"Sure," agreed Elizabeth, "and this can be devastating to what we want. We know we want continuous improvement and also continuous innovation. But blaming people when they make mistakes kills the spirit of innovation. People can't innovate while they're busy protecting themselves. On the other hand, permission to take risks, make mistakes, and challenge the way things have been done in the past opens up people's ability to learn and use their talents. That's why Sandy wanted people here to see mistakes as okay—to be lighthearted about them—to celebrate them, even."

"Interesting," Michael said. "It reminds me of an article I read about encouraging innovation and creativity. I couldn't understand when it mentioned that one company shoots off a cannon every time there's a goof. Now I get it."

"Incidentally," Elizabeth grinned, "if you did go over and correct the spelling on the sign, you'd have some associates here frowning. Since everyone's gotten the message, *m-i-s-t-e-a-k* has become the official spelling of *mistake* in our company."

"You mean they're protective of their right to make errors?"

"In a way, I suppose they are. What do you think happens when people are encouraged to make mistakes that come from innovating and taking risks? Do you think they act more responsibly or less?"

Michael thought about that. He realized he'd come up against a basic belief about people. "I used to think they would act less responsibly. Now I want to think they'd act more responsibly. What have you found?"

"They act with greater responsibility. That's a significant outcome of empowerment. Shifting the definition of a mistake from something bad or wrong to an opportunity to learn encourages people to think and to monitor their own performance. In other words, it empowers them. And what we're learning, again and again, is that when people are empowered, they perform at a higher level. What we must do is hold people accountable for nothing but the best, while recognizing that people must make mistakes to continue to improve."

"I've just figured out something about this matter of 'misteaks,'" Michael said with a smile. "When people are blamed for mistakes, they become self-protective. In fact, they'll cover up mistakes in an effort to avoid blame. This limits the information that flows from the mistake, information everyone could learn from."

"That emphasizes the trust-building element of sharing information," said Elizabeth. "But there are far more practical advantages to the strategy. Want to hear another example?"

Michael nodded. Elizabeth pointed to a coffee mug sitting on a table that had "FOUR HOURS" written on it in large letters.

"Therein lies a miraculous tale based on sharing information and letting people run with their ideas," said Elizabeth. "About a year ago we began to look at our performance. We learned that when customers placed orders, it was taking us three to five days before it was shipped. Until we got that information, we never thought much about it. Now that we had it, we wondered, 'Why should it take so long?' We did some checking and learned that in our industry the typical shipping time for an order was about two days. We wanted to do better than twice the industry average! We began to determine how we could improve.

"Now keep in mind that had we not had the information available to examine, we would not even have been aware of the need for improvement. Also, if some manager had just challenged us to ship orders quicker, we wouldn't have had the commitment."

"I see how that works," said Michael. "The fact that you found it out yourself got you on your own case. And you didn't just know you needed to be better. You decided how much better you needed to be."

"Right. Once we saw the information—especially about how our performance compared to other companies—we knew we had to do something. We made the decision ourselves to change things right here in this department." Michael was noticing the pride Elizabeth took in telling him this story. It was as if he was listening to the owner of the company.

"Within one month of becoming aware of the problem," Elizabeth continued excitedly, "we had cut the shipping time down to the two-day industry average, but we didn't stop there. We knew we could do better. We wanted to see how far we could take it. We continued to track information on our performance. We began to change the way we responded to orders. Every order was now seen as an opportunity to please a customer. Everyone pulled together as a team. Within another month we had cut our shipping time down to less than a day. And now, a year later, our typical shipping time is four hours."

"Four hours! Down from three to five days to four hours—that's incredible!" Michael exclaimed.

"Indeed, it's like a miracle. Amazing results can come from simply giving people the information with which to work, plus the freedom to operate with that information."

Michael began to get excited. "OK, I get it now. People's full talents can't be used by the organization when they don't feel safe and when they don't have information. When they do feel safe, free to experiment, and apprised of all the information management has, they develop the same feelings as owners. Owners are the ones who feel responsible for everything working right in the company, because they have the information to see a more complete picture. Owners don't hold back—they give the success of the company their full attention. When people begin to feel like owners, they begin to act like owners. Now you've got yourself a smarter, more competent organization."

"Right," said Elizabeth, "but let me add one important point: In an empowered organization, position power means very little. Instead we rely on expertise and relationships and on people taking responsibility for their own actions."

"I like that," said Michael. He had a sudden insight about all the great computer technology his company had at its disposal. Up to this point only he and his managers had been using it to share and access sensitive information. The people in the company had all sorts of computer technology available for their use, but he knew that a great deal of information was not at their disposal. He thought, We could make so much better use of our technology if only he and the other managers would share more of the information they used to make decisions. Indeed, maybe by their sharing, others would be encouraged to share more with each other, as well as with the management team.

Michael thought, We are just not making nearly as much use of the technological expertise within our company as we could. He made some notes in his organizer and then looked up at Elizabeth.

"But I still wonder," said Michael thoughtfully. "Does everyone really want to meet this challenge? Don't some people just want to get by?"

"Sure," said Elizabeth. "We've found that a small percentage of people simply don't want the extra responsibility and accountability that comes with having more information. But the vast majority do. It's a matter of reactivating their natural desire."

"You think that people would rather be magnificent than ordinary, right?"

"Exactly," said Elizabeth. "It's just that their desire for magnificence is . . . well . . . dormant. For years in many organizations you were promoted by doing what you were told. 'Don't rock the boat, and you'll get ahead' became a way of life."

"As a result," agreed Michael, "people need to relearn how to take initiative, be responsible and empowered. I'm certainly learning that. Tell me more about how creating autonomy through boundaries makes a difference."

"Of course," agreed Elizabeth. "Why don't we walk over to the cafeteria and get a cup of coffee?"

BOUNDARIES ARE GUIDELINES FOR ACTION

AS THEY strolled along, Elizabeth began to explain how various kinds of structure take on a new meaning in an empowered organization.

"Once people have the information to understand their current situation, boundaries don't seem like constraints but rather guidelines for action. Within our agreed-on boundaries, we have complete autonomy and responsibility to get things done. Take roles and goals, for example. I'm sure Janet Wo talked to you about developing the big picture into little pictures."

"Yes, she did."

"That's important to us, because when it comes to defining roles and goals, our process is like a two-way street. Management and informed people throughout the organization (that is, all of us) work together to develop the big picture, as well as our little pictures. When the vision is clear, everyone knows where their job and their work on individual tasks fits into a bigger perspective."

"Can you give me an example?" asked Michael.

"Have you ever returned to the store a pair of shoes you have worn, and only then discovered they made your feet hurt? The store clerk tells you the best the store can do is give you a store credit for the current price of the shoes, which are now on sale?"

"No, but that would make me angry, I am sure," said Michael.

"Last week," Elizabeth continued, "this happened to me, except the response from the salesperson was exceptional. When I explained my problem, she asked me if there was another style I would prefer more. Unfortunately, there were none, and I just did not have time to consider a lot of options. I just wanted my money back, so she said all right. But when she went to handle the credit, she found the shoes were on sale, and I realized I did not have my receipt. But I knew I had paid more than the sale price. She told me, 'No problem.' She overrode the computer and gave me a cash refund. I was so impressed that I went back a couple of days later and bought two pair of shoes from this person. That was a win for me and for the store, wasn't it? But think about why that worked so well. Not only was that woman a great salesperson, but the training that she'd received provided boundaries that empowered her to help me."

"You mean, within certain guidelines the clerk had control over what to do," said Michael. "The boundaries provided the playing field and the rules, and on that field the salesperson was free to play her own outstanding game."

Elizabeth smiled and nodded.

"That's certainly a new use of terms like *boundaries* and *structure* for me," continued Michael. "In the past, people have become used to working within structure, but the structure's been there to inhibit action, limit thinking and risk taking, and correct mistakes by punishing those responsible."

"You're talking here about a new type of rules and boundaries, one that encourages responsibility, ownership, and empowerment. How do you get people to make that shift? Won't there be all kinds of problems?"

"We certainly had our share of them," Elizabeth answered. "At first we tried eliminating most rules and structure and using slogans to guide us. But we found that didn't work. People were unsure of what to do and afraid to take responsibility for fear of making a mistake. They just cannot go from a controlled environment to complete freedom, autonomy, and responsibility overnight."

"That sounds like what Billy Abrams was telling me about creating self-managed work teams," said Michael. "Managers have to start with strong, clear leadership and gradually move toward more supporting and delegating styles."

"Yes," Elizabeth affirmed. "There's a paradox here. You need rules and structure so that people are comfortable at first during the changeover. But they are not the old rules and structures that dominated hierarchical life. These new boundaries must demonstrate the values that support your empowerment effort. I made a little desk card that many of us keep around as a reminder of this paradox:"

New boundaries help everyone learn to act with responsibility and autonomy.

"Again," said Michael, "I feel the need for an example."

"Good. This example demonstrates our value of 'recovery.' We had shipped some components to a customer, only to find that when the unit was assembled on site, it didn't fit into the space the architect had designed. Our people had met with the architect, visited the building site, and followed the specs to the letter, but somehow a mistake had been made. To correct it would cost us ten thousand dollars, which amounted to our entire profit for the job."

"That's a sticky one," Michael said with a grimace. "What happened?"

"In the past," Elizabeth continued, "we would have put all our energy into identifying who was to blame—the architect, the customer, or someone in our company. But we have a guideline now that says, 'When a mistake is made, first do whatever it takes to recover and then learn from the mistake.' In our training we learned to ask, 'How can we recover so that the customer is happy and so that we get some good learning from this mistake?'"

"That's a great question!" Michael exclaimed. "It's got integrity. How did you come up with it?"

"It came out of the values and dialogue process we all went through in the beginning. We developed a group of rules like this that are basically values questions converted into rules of action."

"If that kind of mistake happened in my company," Michael said, "heads would have rolled after we satisfied the customer. So what happened?"

"We assured the customer that the problem would be fixed. Then while we worked with the contractor and architect to modify the space and the unit itself, we had people on the site charting all the changes, their costs, and the other processes of recovery. Later, a task force met to go over the records to see what we could learn from it."

"How did it all turn out?" Michael asked. "I'm particularly interested in the financial impact on the company."

"We did more than keep a key customer. The way we handled it resulted in a major referral by that client to another string of companies with whom we've been doing business ever since. And we did get our ten thousand dollars worth of learning out of it. The story of that situation resulted in a renewal of commitment throughout the company of getting things right the first time. The situation assured us that we could 'walk our talk' by following our values-based guidelines instead of indulging in 'poor me' or blaming. It demonstrated the capacity of our structure to encourage people's problem-solving instincts, too.

"The key solution in this situation—modifying both the space and the unit—came from a person who had relatively little to do with the project, but her instincts were right on target. Also, the associates who contributed to the recovery project developed managerial thinking and expertise that has since proved invaluable."

That's a lot of payoff, thought Michael. Then he said, "I see now that mistakes are opportunities to improve and use our talents, not times to find fault."

"You know," said Elizabeth, "it's great having the freedom to operate in this new structure. It's also great to find out that every day you can rise to the standards this freedom requires in terms of responsibility and accountability. There's a sign that hangs in what our team calls our 'powwow room' that reminds us of this":

> Empowerment means you have the freedom to act; it also means you are accountable for results.

"You've certainly added to my understanding about information and boundaries, Elizabeth," said Michael. "And I've already taken up too much of your time today."

"It's been my pleasure," said Elizabeth warmly. "I was just about to suggest you talk to someone in Information Services to learn more about self-managed teams. Luis Gomez over there has a story that will interest you. It's about the nervousness their team had about replacing the hierarchy. I'll walk you over.

"One more point," said Elizabeth as they walked to the Information Services Area. "Nothing is static in the empowerment process. The boundaries we've been talking about will continue to widen as people become more empowered. The changes will be noticeable all over the organization. People will define goals for themselves and their peers. They'll suggest new roles and improvements. They'll use their teams far more effectively in some cases than you can expect at first. But I'm going to stop there. Telling you about teams can be Luis's job."

MICHAEL WAS excited to meet with Luis Gomez and learn more about self-managed teams. Luis greeted him with a firm handshake.

Luis began, “So it’s my job to show you more about how teams become the hierarchy. Actually, that’s my favorite subject. Probably the fact that I’m team leader this quarter has something to do with it.”

“Did top management give you some rules that govern your team’s operation?” asked Michael.

“We operate with very few rules from the top,” Luis answered. “In fact, we have only four basic rules, and these were actually developed with all employees involved in a process led by Sandy and her management team. The four rules that guide all our actions are

1. Keep customers first and foremost in our actions.
2. Look after the company’s financial interests.
3. Be flexible in making quality decisions.
4. Keep others in the company informed.”

"But," Michael said, "I've just finished learning from Elizabeth that new rules and boundaries are essential for getting to empowerment."

"That's right, but they're essential mainly at the beginning of the process," Luis said. "We've come a long way on our journey to get where we are today. We started with a lot of external structure and rules. But now those rules come from within our team. Let me tell you how that happened."

"Good," said Michael.

"More than a year ago when we began our journey," Luis said, "Sandy told us that her goal was not only to flatten the organizational pyramid but to turn it upside down for operating decisions."

"What did she mean by 'turn the pyramid upside down for operating decisions'?" asked Michael.

"Suppose you have two phones on your desk, one red and one blue," said Luis. "The red phone is a direct line to the chairman of the board. The blue phone is a direct line to customers. Both phones start ringing at the same time. Which do you answer first?"

Michael paused, then said, "Well, the red phone, of course!"

"Right. And that," said Luis, "is the problem with most organizations. The pyramid is inverted only when it's safe for you to answer the blue phone first."

"I happen to know that your company has gone through a de-layering like we did. But merely reducing the number of management layers does little to change the fundamental way that work gets done in a corporation.

"Without taking some specific steps such as those you've been learning about here, it remains a typical, vertical organization. People continue to look up to their bosses instead of out to customers. Their loyalty is still to the functional fiefdoms in which they work rather than to the overall company and its goals."

"Exactly," Michael replied emphatically, thinking of his own company.

Luis continued, "When people are empowered they don't look up the hierarchy for answers; they take responsibility to solve problems where they occur."

"How did your people respond to this new responsibility?" asked Michael.

"At first, when people began to realize that they had more responsibility, many of them acted like they didn't want it. There were feelings left over from the old days when the attitude was 'That's not my job.' I remember hearing people say, 'If we're gonna be bosses, we should be getting more pay.' Handling this resistance to change was one of the things we had to learn. It was critical to our empowerment efforts."

"What was the first thing you did to help change attitudes?" Michael asked.

"Sandy kept preaching the belief that decisions had to be made at the lowest level of the organization—that is, at the front line."

"Don't you mean 'at the highest level of the organization when the pyramid is inverted'?"

"Good catch," laughed Luis. "For people to take on the responsibility for these important decisions, they were going to need new skills and different ways to operate. In short, they had to learn to act in responsible, decision-making teams."

"How did people take to that?"

"They were confused. On the one hand it sounded good, but they didn't know what it meant. Neither did the managers. Everyone became discouraged and confused about what to do next, because they had never done this before, either. It was a very frustrating period of time for everyone. It became clear you could not just announce empowerment and expect it to magically occur."

"That's what I've done," said Michael, reflecting on the recent happenings at his company. "How did you pull out of this mess? Before I came to see Sandy and all of you, I was ready to throw in the towel and give up."

"We almost gave up ourselves," said Luis, "but then two things happened. First, Sandy didn't give up. She just persisted and kept talking to us as if we were all managers. A simple example is the *asking memo* she began to use."

"Asking memo?"

"You know how it goes in the typical unempowered organization: A memo comes down from on high saying we all need to start to save electricity or paper or some darn thing, and people stand around and look at each other, smile, and say, 'R-i-i-i-ght.' Then the manager comes out of his or her office and starts giving out orders about how it's to be done. Everybody feels like a naughty kid getting a lecture."

"That sounds like what I've seen, and done, all my life," sighed Michael."

"That's a *telling memo*," nodded Luis. "An *asking memo* is different. Take the case of the problem of saving resources. Sandy's memo would start out with the pertinent cost information, broken down to include the department's portion of the problem. The language of the memo would be short and sweet—no pep talk like, 'Let's all get behind this effort.' It would be written simply, as if the readers needed this information so they could make decisions about it. When people in our department received one of those early asking memos from Sandy, they looked at each other and then read the memo again. It was obvious that a departmental decision had to be made.

"It was just as obvious that no one was going to make it for us," Luis continued. "Pretty soon a dialogue would start. People would suggest things they could do. Then they'd decide what they *would* do."

"Early version of a team meeting," Michael put in. "How about carrying out the decision?"

"A snap," replied Luis. "Since the group had dealt with the problem on its own, the group 'owned' the solution. You know the way it is whenever you have a joint agreement with somebody. You both feel willing to carry it out and also to tell the other person if he or she goofs."

Michael nodded. "But I'm wondering about something. As you were developing these self-managed teams, what was the function of the managers?"

"That leads into the second thing that helped pull us through a period of high dissatisfaction and discouragement—training! Managers knew they should be behaving differently and so did their team members, but nobody had a clue what to do until Sandy required us all to go to team skills training."

"Required you to go to training?" echoed Michael.

"Yes," said Luis. "Sandy sees training not as an option but as a value. She made team skills training a requirement for everybody. She said that once you're scheduled for training, you cannot cancel it for any reason other than for a personal emergency. She said if we were ever tempted to pull someone from training, we should call her, and she'd work the person's shift."

Luis excused himself for a moment to respond to a question from a teammate.

Michael wondered what Luis meant by required training. He thought about how training had worked in his organization and in other organizations he'd seen. People were scheduled for training, then were pulled out by supervisors because of some bureaucratic crisis—the vice president was making a visit, or more people were needed to take inventory. Sandy Fitzwilliam was obviously a leader committed to training as a way to bring about needed change.

When Luis returned, Michael asked him how many requests Sandy got to work people's shifts.

"Not one," Luis answered. "When top managers are squarely behind the training of teams, it really smoothes the way. Remember the second step to empowerment?"

"Clear boundaries lead to empowerment," said Michael. "I see. But what about all the dissatisfaction and discouragement you said people were experiencing? How did they work through it?"

"It took a while," said Luis. "In our training we learned that groups, like individuals, go through predictable stages of development. They need different kinds of leadership at each stage."

"Tell me more about the group stages," Michael said, once again getting out his organizer.

"When a group first forms, members are typically enthusiastic, but they don't know how they're going to operate or who's going to play what role. That's called the *orientation stage*, and it's a time when a team needs strong, clear leadership. Someone has to set the agendas and organize the team's efforts.

"We didn't do that initially, and our teams quickly moved into the second stage of development, the *dissatisfaction stage.* The reality of working as a team always seems to be more difficult than team members expect. In the training sessions, we learned that teams in dissatisfaction need continued strong, clear leadership. But they also need support—someone to listen to their concerns and cheerlead for any progress made. We learned that, while this dissatisfaction stage is uncomfortable, it's a critical stage for ultimately becoming a self-managing team. It was in this dissatisfaction stage that we began to experiment with a role we still use today called the 'team coordinator.'"

Michael said, "We use team leaders in my company, but I have an idea you mean something a little different."

Luis nodded and said, "During the initial stages of our teams, the team coordinator, in many ways, acts like a manager. After a team moves into *resolution*—the third stage of team development, when members begin to learn to work together—we start to rotate the role of team coordinator among team members. The role of the coordinator is to support and facilitate the team.

"Also, it's important that team members understand what's going on in other areas," continued Luis. "So the coordinator attends weekly meetings of other departments and reports back to the team. This process supports one of the organization's key values—cross-training and cross-utilization. Most of the decisions are made as a team, but the coordinator does the detail part, handling most of the paper work, scheduling people for vacation time, and so forth.

"The coordinator also trains the next person in rotation. We found that the team coordinator role becomes less critical as the final *production stage* of development is reached. A self-managed team acts to direct and support individual efforts itself. Again and again we learned the value of diversity as a real asset for dealing with the complex problems we face today. And when I talk about diversity, I'm not just talking about race and sex but also cultural background, as well as diversity of abilities, skills, and opinions. We found that by drawing upon the unique skills, perspectives and knowledge of our team members, we developed far better solutions to our problems."

"So as people's capabilities and contributions increase, the whole becomes greater than the sum of its parts," Michael summarized. "But I know that dealing with diversity can be difficult. It's much easier if everyone thinks alike. Haven't there ever been times when your teams just blew it?"

"Oh, sure," replied Luis. "Many times teams have learned the hard way. They've failed to utilize their resources and explore differences of opinion and tried to railroad decisions through."

"What happened?"

"It backfired. Next time the team had to decide something, those members whose ideas were ignored were uncooperative."

"So team development really involves using a lot of human relations skills."

"Absolutely. Any time we're to make a decision on a complex matter, we have to make sure each person has an opportunity to express his or her opinions and concerns. We do this not only to be fair but so that each individual's talents can be brought to bear on the problem."

"When a team has reached the production stage, what is it able to do?" asked Michael.

"Over the last year or so, our teams have used a discussion series titled *Power Up for Team Results* to provide follow-up to the training and to guide us through the stages of becoming empowered teams. Gradually, we have taken on the responsibility for more and more important decisions. A number of teams are now at a point where they actually do all or many of the functions traditionally viewed as the job of management—such as hiring and disciplining, performance evaluations, allocation of resources, quality assurance. These teams have really replaced the old management hierarchy."

"Amazing!" exclaimed Michael. He shook his head thoughtfully.

"What's wrong?" asked Luis.

"Several times today I've been faced with the evidence that empowerment really works, but it challenges my old beliefs."

"Hey, join the club," laughed Luis. "Most managers would say that if you trust people to be responsible for performing these functions and monitoring themselves, you're just asking for trouble. Maybe that would have been true of individuals the way they were accustomed to being treated under the old command-and-control management model. But when you empower people with information and boundaries and then train them to operate in self-managed teams, it's different.

"Since we committed ourselves to empowerment, I've come to see that the people in our company were a vastly underutilized resource. When they understand that you're trusting them to use their brains and their abilities, their own sense of responsibility kicks in. It's as if they've just been waiting for a chance to view the organization as their own, so they could improve it. Combine this intelligence and energy with a shared commitment to serving the customer, and you've got something really powerful!

"What's more," Luis continued, "we keep getting better and better, and people continue to grow and develop new skills and abilities."

"In fact, if people are not continuing to grow and develop, then we find that they just don't seem to fit here anymore, and they wind up leaving. As long as people want to continue to grow, continue to develop, and continue to stretch themselves, they have a place here—they really fit. And that means we wind up having an organization that is profitable in many ways.

"I've developed a list of all the benefits of self-managed teams":

Benefits of Self-Managed Teams

- Increased job satisfaction
- Attitude change from "have to" to "want to"
- Greater employee commitment
- Better communication between employees and management
- More efficient decision-making process
- Improved quality
- Reduced operating costs
- More profitable organization

"And for all those payoffs to occur," replied Michael, "your self-managed teams need to have a great deal of information. Now I understand further why information sharing is the first key to empowerment."

"You're absolutely right. And the need for information sharing continues to grow," explained Luis. "We have had to develop better mechanisms for recording information and for making it available to more people. One of the beauties of today's computer technology is that it allows us to put information into a form that's readily available to everyone through our company network. Everybody knows what's going on all the time. You see, for teams to be responsible, they demand a tremendous amount of information, more than they've ever had.

"We've also found as we've operated," Luis continued, "that our team members are asking for only the information that's really useful to them. That keeps us from being inundated with requests for information that they'll never use.

"That means we don't have to prepare as many reports as before, but the reports we do prepare convey important information to our teams. Since teams are thinking about the importance of what they do, they're continually looking for better ways to do things and more ways to utilize the skills and abilities they have. After all, this is their organization, isn't it?"

"Fascinating," said Michael. "I'm finally getting a handle on how empowerment works and the impact it can have on organizational performance."

"Great! I'm glad I could help," smiled Luis.

Michael thanked Luis and headed out thinking, I'll stop by Sandy's office and see if she has any final words of wisdom before I start my real and enlightened journey to the Land of Empowerment.

PERSIST IN YOUR BELIEF IN EMPOWERMENT

AS MICHAEL walked back to Sandy's office he was feeling good about all he had learned. It seemed like a long time ago when he had been dragging his feet.

"Well, are you ready to go?" Sandy smiled as she greeted him.

"I think so. Your associates have been very helpful, and I've learned a great deal about empowerment. Implementing the three keys sounds like quite a challenge but also a great gift to everyone in our company. I hope we can make it work for us."

"There is no doubt that you will need persistence in your belief that empowerment will work."

"Particularly with the last key—replacing hierarchical thinking with self-managed teams," said Michael. "Information sharing got me at first, but the role of teams seems even tougher."

"That's the part that always makes managers doubt the whole process," Sandy replied.

"When the inevitable confusion and dissatisfaction stage of the journey sets in, it must seem so out of control," Michael said in a pained tone.

"Yes! Know why?" Sandy asked. "Because if you are going to be held accountable, you want to be in control."

"Right!"

"But the reality is that if you're going to empower people, you have to give up control and still remain accountable."

"Very scary for a manager."

"Especially when the organization gets to this stage of confusion and lack of leadership regarding next steps."

"The team skills training sounds like it helps," said Michael. "Just knowing that dissatisfaction is a natural, predictable stage of group development probably puts things in perspective."

"That's why I required the training," Sandy said. "I had tried before to empower people but didn't know the inevitability or severity of the dissatisfaction stage. When confusion and disillusionment began to occur, I was as scared as anyone. I was afraid I'd created a monster that none of us would be able to control. I wanted to head for the hills and abdicate."

"But you didn't, obviously."

"No, but I've seen a lot of managers do just that, and empowerment often goes by the wayside."

"How did you hang in there?"

"Naive enthusiasm, probably," she laughed. "I kept reminding myself and everyone else that people really did want to be empowered, and it could make a performance difference in our organization. But I want to tell you, many a night I sat at my desk staring into space and wondering what I had gotten myself into. The Land of Empowerment seemed far away. I sensed a leadership vacuum in the organization. Here I was asking people to make a major change in their way of relating to each other, but neither I nor the other managers knew what guidance to provide. It was a very frustrating period for everyone."

"What happened?" quizzed Michael.

"Gradually something interesting began to happen. It's like in the movies when the hero is on his last leg and you can't figure out how he's going to make it."

"But he always does!"

"Sure. That's what makes a good movie. The solution comes from some source you hadn't expected. That's what happened in our empowerment experience. Right in the midst of the leadership vacuum, flickering lights of empowerment began to shine from colleagues on the teams. Teams began to make important action decisions, individuals risked speaking out with suggestions, and managers acted in ways to facilitate decisions rather than make them. I think the discussion booklets that the teams were using helped more than they or I realized.

"Out of the discomfort of the leadership vacuum, the very empowerment we wanted was born. The information sharing, new boundaries, and skills training for teams began to pay off."

"I don't know if I could have hung in there," reflected Michael.

"That's why it's important to understand that the empowerment journey begins with direction during the orientation stage and requires you to add support to your efforts as natural dissatisfaction sets in. Any wavering from the vision at that time could be disastrous."

"So staying in the middle of the fray can speed up the movement to self-managed teams, even when you are unsure what to do to help?"

"That's it," Sandy said. "When it seems no one has the answer, people come forward in ways that can astonish you. And you can naturally step back to let their empowerment shine, while you eventually become a team member with your colleagues."

"The key seems to be to stick to your beliefs," said Michael as he wrote some thoughts in his organizer.

"That's the only way your beliefs can become reality, but sometimes it can be very scary."

"Well, you said in the beginning that the journey to the Land of Empowerment would not be easy," said Michael. "I understand that thoroughly now, but I'm still ready to go."

"Good luck," Sandy said as they walked to the door.

"I'll need it," said Michael. "And you'll be hearing from me."

"Any time," Sandy replied as she waved good-bye to him. "And remember," she added, "it does work—if you stick with it."

MICHAEL SPENT that evening collecting his thoughts and preparing to begin the empowerment journey with his organization.

He spent a good deal of time arranging and rearranging his notes into a coherent pattern that he could use to explain what he had learned.

Finally, he came up with something he called the *Empowerment Game Plan.* This game plan summarized the three keys to empowerment. He used arrows to show that you start with Share Accurate Information and then bring in Create Autonomy through Boundaries and Replace Hierarchical Thinking with Self-managed Teams to create a three-pronged approach to creating a culture of empowerment. He decided he would give copies to everyone in his organization. It looked like this:

THE EMPOWERMENT GAME PLAN

Start with—

Share Accurate Information with Everyone

- Share performance information about the company; help people understand the business.
- Build trust through sharing.
- Set up self-monitoring possibilities.
- View mistakes as learning opportunities.
- Break down hierarchical thinking; help people behave as owners.

Then

Create Autonomy through Boundaries

- Clarify the big and little pictures.
- Clarify goals and roles.
- Define values and rules that underlie actions.
- Create rules and procedures that support empowerment.
- Provide needed training.
- Hold people accountable for results.

And

Replace Hierarchical Thinking with Self-Managed Teams

- Provide direction and skills training for empowered teams.
- Provide support and encouragement for change.
- Use diversity as a team asset.
- Gradually give control to the teams.
- Recognize there will be some rough times.

Over the next few months, Michael and his company traveled along their own unique journey toward the Land of Empowerment. At first, he made periodic calls to Sandy Fitzwilliam for advice and feedback. Over time, however, as his confidence grew, he and his associates became engaged in their own process of developing an empowered organization. Despite setbacks and some times when they all wanted to just give up, they persisted. By Michael's knowing and sharing with everyone that such hard times and reactions were to be expected, they were able to stick to the task and continue to use the three keys to move through all the stages of change and associated difficulties. Eventually they achieved their goal of creating an empowered organization where everyone could use and develop talents that both engaged them and achieved astonishing results for the organization.

Just as Sandy had acted as a guide for Michael, he found himself counseling other executives who were moving through their own journeys. Again and again he heard himself say,

"Empowerment isn't magic. It consists of a few simple steps and a lot of persistence."

EPILOGUE

ABOUT A YEAR later, Michael ran into Sandy at a business conference and began to tell her more about his experiences with creating a culture of empowerment and helping others do the same. They wound up talking for quite awhile, as Michael shared what he had learned about the process of moving to the Land of Empowerment.

Michael said, "You know, Sandy, you told me how challenging the journey would be and it certainly was, but I now know a way to help others better appreciate what happens."

"Oh, tell me about it," replied Sandy.

"Well, it really comes from what you told me about the stages of team development. You told me that teams go through three stages before they reach the production stage of being high performing, empowered teams: orientation, dissatisfaction, and resolution. I think it helps to think of the change to empowerment as occurring in three rather similar stages. First is *Starting and Orienting the Journey*. As you use the first key to empowerment—Share Accurate

Information—people tend to get excited about the possibilities. They want to know more and more about the need for the change to empowerment. And the more information you share, the more they get excited and the more they want to take responsibility for impacting results."

Sandy interrupted, "I know what you mean. It's amazing to watch the energy grow in people just from sharing accurate and timely information they have not seen and used before."

"Absolutely," said Michael.

"But, Michael, what always disappoints me is how this energy is so hard to keep going. My experience has always been that as people learn more through information sharing, their fears also rise. They get concerned about how the change to empowerment will affect them personally. They wonder if they will be able to handle the increased responsibility that goes with empowerment."

"Exactly," replied Michael. "And that leads directly to the second and most difficult stage in the process, the stage where so many people want to give up and where some do give up. I call it the stage of *Change and Discouragement.* It's a lot like the team stage of dissatisfaction, just more broad-based."

"I know exactly what you mean, Michael, but tell me more of your thinking. Let's compare experiences."

"During this stage people often are trying to change but they get discouraged. Their personal concerns become stronger, and they ask for more specifics about how to implement the change in culture. They want the security of specific steps to take to be successful in the change and to not get hurt in the process. The fear of failure and the associated consequences in the old hierarchical culture are very real for people, and this fear inhibits their taking empowered action."

"Michael, that's a brilliant way to put it, but you know what? My experience tells me it is very hard to spell out specific steps in the change process. Every situation is different."

"Right, Sandy, but just by acknowledging the discouragement and deciding on little steps of progress, while sharing more information and getting the teams more involved, people are able to move through this valley of doubt—as an informed team. Remember how you told me about the leadership vacuum that occurs during the journey?"

"Of course," said Sandy.

"Well, I have learned that's what this stage is all about. It is incredibly uncomfortable for everyone, especially the people on the frontline who are afraid of what will happen if they fail. In fact that is why it is critical in this stage to begin using information sharing in reverse. Managers need to focus much more on *listening* as information flows from employees toward the managers—employees tell us what their concerns are if we will just listen."

"Good point, Michael. I think this second stage of the change is full of strange paradoxes that only make sense in hindsight."

"Yeah, yeah, Sandy. I think it's the most amazing paradox that happens when you deal effectively with the issues in this stage. I mean, it's just amazing. To deal with this fear people have during *Change and Discouragement*, managers must *widen* the boundaries to create more autonomy and responsibility. People at this stage have more ability than they realize, and they can only come to appreciate their ability if you give them a chance to use more of it by widening the boundaries."

"Michael, you are so right! You are so right. It definitely makes it easier for people to change if they understand that the journey involves these stages and if they know how to use the three keys to empowerment differently in each stage to address the unique issues that arise. But tell me more about what you have learned about the third stage of change."

"Right! The third stage is like the light at the end of the tunnel. I call it *Adopting and Refining Empowerment.* People can now see the value of empowerment, at least some can see it. And those who do want to use their knowledge and experience to make it better. They want everyone to get on board because they have gained a sense of how rewarding it is to be empowered."

Sandy interrupted, "Sort of makes empowerment personal, doesn't it? Empowerment is not just for the company; it's a way for each person in the organization to feel engaged and magnificent."

"Couldn't agree with you more, Sandy. But I think the challenge at this point in the process is to keep it going just a little longer. The third stage is not the destination yet, though it is getting really close."

"Now I could not agree with you more. I have seen some companies drop the ball by not keeping the pressure on all the way to the finish line. I think that at this third stage the three keys to empowerment take on new meaning and application. Information sharing really comes from all directions—from everyone to everyone. The boundaries for autonomy are quite wide and are driven by people throughout the organization. And the teams really start to run the show."

Michael added, "You better believe it. The three keys are really working in synergy to keep the empowerment process going and going and going!"

"And as I just said, people are feeling the sense of engagement that only comes from being empowered.

Sandy and Michael continued to talk and agreed to try to write down their ideas for others to read and use. They wanted to generate excitement and knowledge in as many people as possible about this thing called *empowerment*. They wanted everyone to know that

The Process of Changing to
Empowerment
Is Not Impossible!
But it helps to know how to use
The three keys to empowerment differently
In each of the three stages in the journey.

For more detailed information about using the three keys to empowerment to address the issues in each of the three stages in the change to empowerment, see the book *The Three Keys to Empowerment: Release the Power in People for Astonishing Results* by Ken Blanchard, John P. Carlos, and Alan Randolph (Berrett-Koehler Publishers, 1999).

In addition, see the discussion series for teams to guide themselves on their own journey to empowerment, titled *Power Up for Team Results,* also by Ken Blanchard, John P. Carlos, and Alan Randolph with Peter B. Grazier (Berrett-Koehler Publishers, 2000).

Acknowledgments

There are so many people to thank and acknowledge for the learnings that led to this book. Inevitably, we will leave out some people, but we will do our best to be as complete as possible. To cover as many bases as possible (without writing another book), we offer thank-you's to a special group of people who have been most helpful in the formulation of our ideas. We also offer acknowledgments to a much wider list of people and companies we have learned from as they reacted to earlier drafts of our book. To all, we wish to express our sincerest appreciation. We know they will recognize their contributions throughout the book.

Thank you to the following companies and people in them who have been courageous in their pioneering efforts to empower people and organizations:

Mary Andrulewicz, Jack Kent, and all the business unit leaders at Sheppard-Pratt Hospital

George Clifton (retired) and many others in the East Bay Region of Pacific Gas and Electric Company

Ron Floto, Dennis Carter, Lewis Payne, the top management team, and the many district and store managers at Kash 'N' Karry Stores

Jeanne Gruner and the Performance Management Task Force at Household International

Tom Jackson, Mike Squilante, Jeff Beck, and a host of others from Advanta Corporation

Stephan Sebastian with Cargill

Sally Heinz at The St. Paul Companies

Mark Robbins and David Heckman at Robbins-Gioia, Inc.

Lanny Julian and the amazing field staff of Ambassador Cards

David Liddle of Circle K Stores (U.K.)

Jim Pantelidas, Ron McIntosh, Gordon Olitch, and Wolfgang Greogry of Petro-Canada

Irv Rule and Matthew Reimann of Seimens Medical Systems, plus John Donnelly, formerly of Siemens Medical Systems

Ralph Stayer of Johnsonville Foods for showing us and many others the way to create real empowerment

Steve Wachter and the managers and employees of General Electric Information Services

George Wilson and many others at Florida Power and Light, plus Jo-Anne Pitera and Barbara Dabney, formerly at Florida Power and Light

Acknowledgments to the following people who read drafts of the book before it was originally published and shared openly of their experiences in giving us feedback on the book:

Barbara Balter with the Robert B. Balter Company

Joe Bode formerly with Black and Decker Corporation

Don J. Carlos and Bill Carlos, brothers emeritus

Arnie Cole with the U.S. Army

John Coleman with CSX Corporation

Bruce Dalgleish with General Mills Restaurants

Mike Gill with Americom Cellular (now Solectron)

Charles J. Loew with Motorola University

Mike Louden with Louden Associates

Rick Miller with the Boys and Girls Club of Phoenix

Mike Perry with the E. I. Du Pont Company

Al Price with the Mauna Kea Beach Hotel

Joe Raymond with the Georgia Academy

Lou Reymann formerly with Shimadzu Scientific Instruments

Al Schneider with the Federal Communications Commission

Julie Seeherman with Venture Stores

Tom Walczykowski with the FBI

We would like to express our sincere thanks to Carlita Anthony-Mines, Valerie Hall, Michele Jansen, Harry Paul, and Eleanor Terndrup, for producing the original version of this book in a most efficient manner and to Bob Nelson for his helpful feedback and editing.

We would also like to thank Margret McBride, our agent, and Steven Piersanti, editor at Berrett-Koehler, for their encouragement and energy in publishing this book.

In addition, we owe an intellectual debt to many of our colleagues at The Ken Blanchard Companies, especially Eunice Parisi-Carew and Don Carew for sharing their knowledge about team development; Jesse Stoner and Drea Zigarmi for their thinking about creating a compelling vision; Pat Zigarmi for new insights on Situational Leadership II; and Dev Ogle for sharing his knowledge of continuous improvement and strategic thinking.

Most important, we would like to thank our wives—Marjorie Blanchard, Lynne Carlos, and Ruth Anne Randolph—whose support and challenging questions helped us refine this book to a high level of value for our readers.

Ken Blanchard would also like to acknowledge the impact a visit with C. O. Woody, Rita Craig, and some of the good folks from the Power Generation Business Unit of Florida Power and Light had on his thinking about self-directed teams. In particular, a big One Minute Praising goes to Rick Beil, Eddie Childs, Mary Polk, and Debra Shultz-Robinson, who have been involved in self-directed teams at the Turkey Point Fossil and Cutler Plants. Their experience has been heartwarming and successful.

John Carlos would also like to praise the following people:

Mike Vance—my phantom mentor for over twenty years

Rick and Ester Miller—for standing by me when many didn't

Lino and Kelly Antunes, Andee and Todd Oleno—my children, who have always been an inspiration

Gordon Dolan—a good friend and colleague

First Sergeant Harold J. Merton—who first taught me about leadership

Alan Randolph would also like to praise these fine folks:

Barry Posner and Jackie Schmidt-Posner for their constant friendship and colleagueship

Dan Costello for his support and encouragement

John Hatfield for his support and friendship

Father Vincent Dwyer for his early inspiration

My children—Ashley, Shannon, and Liza, who inspire me to be empowered and to empower them

About the Authors

Ken Blanchard has had tremendous impact on the day-to-day management of people and companies. As a writer in the field of management, his impact has been far-reaching. His One Minute Manager Library, which includes *The One Minute Manager* (1982), *Putting the One Minute Manager to Work* (1984), *Leadership and the One Minute Manager* (1985), *The One Minute Manager Balances Work and Life* (2000), *The One Minute Manager Meets the Monkey* (1989), and *The One Minute Manager Builds High Performing Teams* (1990, 2000), has collectively sold more than twelve million copies and has been translated into more than twenty languages.

Ken has also coauthored several other best-selling books: *Management of Organizational Behavior* (with Dr. Paul Hersey), a classic textbook now in its sixth edition; *The Power of Ethical Management* (1988, with Dr. Norman Vincent Peale); *Raving Fans: A Revolutionary Approach to Customer Service* (1992, with Sheldon Bowles); *Everyone's a Coach* (1995, with Don Shula): *Gung Ho!* (with Sheldon Bowles, 1998);

and *High Five!* (with Sheldon Bowles, Don Carew, and Eunice Parisi-Carew, 2001). *We Are the Beloved* (1994) highlights Ken's spiritual journey.

Over the last few years, Ken has teamed with John P. Carlos and Alan Randolph on several projects on the topic of empowerment: *Empowerment Takes More Than a Minute* (1st ed., 1996), *The Three Keys to Empowerment: Release the Power within People for Astonishing Results* (1999), and *Power Up for Team Results* (2000, with an additional coauthor, Peter B. Grazier).

Ken is chief spiritual officer (CSO) of The Ken Blanchard Companies, a full-service management consulting and training company that he founded in 1979 with his wife, Marjorie Blanchard. He maintains a visiting lectureship at Cornell University, where he also serves as Trustee Emeritus. The Blanchards live in San Diego and have two children, Debbie and Scott; plus a son-in-law, Humberto; a daughter-in-law, Chris; and two grandchildren, Kurtis and Kyle.

John P. Carlos is a highly skilled management consultant, trainer, and motivational speaker. With twenty-five years of hands-on experience as a manager and trainer, his knowledge of organizational and management development, succession planning, team empowerment, customer service, leadership training, and managing diversity is considered to be at the leading edge of today's technology. John specializes in organization and people development, empowering teams and developing companies to deliver legendary customer service.

As a speaker, he is best known for his humorous and insightful real-life stories and his ability to focus people on their own behavior. His years of experience include private, for-profit, and nonprofit organizations, convenience stores, hotels and resorts, and residential treatment schools for adjudicated, hard-to-place teenagers. For ten years he was the director of training for Circle K, a retail food company with more than five thousand outlets worldwide. He heads his own consulting group and is a senior consulting partner with The Ken Blanchard Companies.

John has worked very closely with Ken Blanchard and Alan Randolph on the three empowerment projects: *Empowerment Takes More Than a Minute* (1st ed., 1996), *The Three Keys to Empowerment: Release the Power within People for Astonishing Results* (1999), and *Power Up for Team Results* (2000, with an additional coauthor, Peter B. Grazier).

John received a bachelor's degree in business and an M.B.A. from Columbia Pacific University. He now lives with his wife, Lynne Carlos, in Phoenix, Arizona. His two grown daughters, Kelly and Andee, and his sons-in-law, Todd and Lino, also live in Arizona.

Alan Randolph is an internationally respected and highly accomplished management educator and consultant. He has consulted on management and organizational skills and issues with domestic and international organizations in both public and private sectors, for over twenty years. His specialties include empowerment, project planning and management, performance management, leadership, customer service, and team building. As a seminar presenter and speaker, he is relaxed, clear, and to the point.

Alan is professor of management at the University of Baltimore's Merrick School of Business and a senior consulting partner with The Ken Blanchard Companies. He has published a variety of articles in such practitioner and academic journals as *The Harvard Business Review*, *Sloan Management Review*, *The Academy of Management Journal*, and *Organizational Dynamics*. He is coauthor of several books, including *Getting the Job Done: Managing Project Teams and Task Forces for Success* (1992, with Barry Posner) and *The Organization Game* (1993, with Robert Miles and Edward Kemery).

More recently he collaborated with Ken Blanchard and John P. Carlos on three projects on empowerment: *Empowerment Takes More Than a Minute* (1st ed., 1996), *The Three Keys to Empowerment: Release the Power within People for Astonishing Results* (1999), and *Power Up for Team Results* (2000, with an additional coauthor, Peter B. Grazier). Alan has also published several research and practitioner articles on empowerment, most notably in *Organizational Dynamics.*

Alan holds a bachelor's degree in industrial engineering from the Georgia Institute of Technology, a master's degree in personnel and industrial relations, and a Ph.D. degree in business administration from the University of Massachusetts, Amherst. He and his wife, Ruth Anne Randolph (also a senior consulting partner with The Ken Blanchard Companies), live in Baltimore, Maryland. They have three daughters, Ashley, Shannon, and Liza.

Services Available

The Ken Blanchard Companies is a full-service consulting and training company in the areas of empowerment, leadership, teamwork, performance management, customer service, quality management, ethics, and visioning.

Empowerment is included in a long line of key leadership concepts that Ken Blanchard and his colleagues have made easy to understand and accessible to managers in both the private and public sectors. Based on research and consultation with a wide variety of companies and dating back over fifteen years, the empowerment concepts have been developed to assist managers in guiding their people and organizations to the Land of Empowerment. The keys to empowerment make significant links to many other topics that have been developed by the Blanchard team: Situational Leadership II; Building High Performing Teams; Gung Ho!, Creating Your Organization's Future; Total Quality Leadership; Situational Self Leadership; and Partnering for Performance Management.

The Ken Blanchard Companies offers consulting, training, and speaking services and a complete product line of videos and print material designed to enhance individual and organizational learning and change.

To learn more about how we can show you how to empower yourself, your people and organization, please contact us at

The Ken Blanchard Companies
125 State Place
Escondido, CA 92029
(800) 728-6000 or (619) 489-5005
www.kenblanchard.com

You may contact Ken Blanchard and John Carlos directly through the Blanchard Companies office in Escondido at these numbers. Alan Randolph can be contacted directly at his Baltimore office at (410) 321-8231.

You may also contact the authors directly via e-mail as follows:

Ken Blanchard, ken.blanchard@kenblanchard.com
John P. Carlos, mpowering@aol.com
Alan Randolph, alanran@earthlink.net

An Invitation:

In our quest for continued learning about empowerment and the journey to get there, we invite you to send us stories describing your questions, experiences, and insights about empowerment. Send your comments to

Alan Randolph
The Empowerment File
1409 Locust Avenue
Baltimore, MD 21204

Berrett-Koehler Publishers

Berrett-Koehler is an independent publisher of books, periodicals, and other publications at the leading edge of new thinking and innovative practice on work, business, management, leadership, stewardship, career development, human resources, entrepreneurship, and global sustainability.

Since the company's founding in 1992, we have been committed to supporting the movement toward a more enlightened world of work by publishing books, periodicals, and other publications that help us to integrate our values with our work and work lives, and to create more humane and effective organizations.

We have chosen to focus on the areas of work, business, and organizations, because these are central elements in many people's lives today. Furthermore, the work world is going through tumultuous changes, from the decline of job security to the rise of new structures for organizing people and work. We believe that change is needed at all levels—individual, organizational, community, and global—and our publications address each of these levels.

We seek to create new lenses for understanding organizations, to legitimize topics that people care deeply about but that current business orthodoxy censors or considers secondary to bottom-line concerns, and to uncover new meaning, means, and ends for our work and work lives.

See next pages for other publications from Berrett-Koehler

Spread the word!

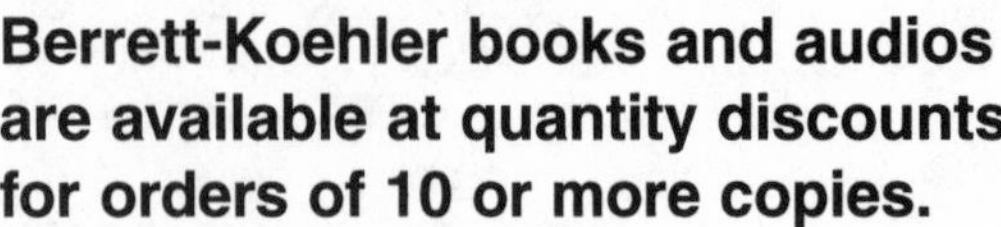

Berrett-Koehler books and audios are available at quantity discounts for orders of 10 or more copies.

Empowerment Takes More Than a Minute

2nd Edition

Ken Blanchard, John P. Carlos, and Alan Randolph

Paperback, 145 pages
ISBN 1-57675-153-8
Item #51538-379 $12.95

To find out about discounts on orders of 10 or more copies for individuals, corporations, institutions, and organizations, please call us toll-free at (800) 929-2929.

To find out about our discount programs for resellers, please contact our Special Sales department at (415) 288-0260; Fax: (415) 362-2512. Or email us at bkpub@bkpub.com.

Berrett-Koehler Publishers
PO Box 565, Williston, VT 05495-9900
Call toll-free! **800-929-2929** 7 am-12 midnight
Or fax your order to 802-864-7627
For fastest service order online: **www.bkconnection.com**